The Massey Lectures Se...

The Massey Lectures are co-sponsored by CBC Radio, House of Anansi Press, and Massey College in the University of Toronto. The series was created in honour of the Right Honourable Vincent Massey, former governor general of Canada, and was inaugurated in 1961 to provide a forum on radio where major contemporary thinkers could address important issues of our time.

This book comprises the 1987 Massey Lectures, "Compassion and Solidarity," broadcast in November 1987 as part of CBC Radio's *Ideas* series. The producer of the series was Marilyn Powell; the executive producer was Bernie Lucht.

Gregory Baum

Born in Berlin to a Jewish family in 1923, and brought up nominally Christian, Gregory Baum came to Canada in 1940. He became a Roman Catholic and joined the Augustinian Order in 1974. Baum soon rose to prominence as an eminent theologian, but after differences with his order, chose to resign from the priesthood in 1976. He taught at St. Michael's College, University of Toronto until 1986, and then moved on to his current position as a teacher of religious studies at McGill University. Baum was one of the experts chosen to prepare documents for the Vatican II Council in 1962. However, his sharp criticism of the Vatican stand on sexual ethics caused him to be regarded as a maverick and a renegade. He is still at odds with his church over some of its views, and supports birth control, the marriage of priests, and the ordination of women. Baum is an Officer of the Order of Canada and has received seven honorary doctorates from universities in Canada and the United States.

COMPASSION *and* SOLIDARITY

GREGORY BAUM

Compassion *and* Solidarity

THE CHURCH FOR OTHERS

ANANSI

First published in 1987 by CBC Enterprises
Published in 1992 by House of Anansi Press Ltd.

This edition published in 2006 by
House of Anansi Press Inc.
110 Spadina Avenue, Suite 801
Toronto, ON, M5V 2K4
Tel. 416-363-4343
Fax 416-363-1017
www.anansi.ca

Distributed in Canada by
HarperCollins Canada Ltd.
1995 Markham Road
Scarborough, ON, M1B 5M8
Toll free tel. 1-800-387-0117

Distributed in the United States by
Publishers Group West
1700 Fourth Street
Berkeley, CA 94710
Toll free tel. 1-800-788-3123

CBC and Massey College logos used with permission

House of Anansi Press is committed to protecting our natural environment. As part
of our efforts, this book is printed on Rolland Enviro paper: it contains 100%
post-consumer recycled fibres, is acid-free, and is processed chlorine-free.

10 09 08 07 06   2 3 4 5 6

LIBRARY AND ARCHIVES CANADA CATALOGUING IN PUBLICATION DATA

Baum, Gregory, 1923–
Compassion and solidarity; the church for others

(CBC Massey lectures series; 1987)

ISBN-13: 978-0-88784-532-1
ISBN-10: 0-88784-532-0

1. Liberation theology. 2. Social justice. 3. Church and
social problems. 4. Solidarity — Religious aspects —
Christianity. I. Title. II. Series

BT83.57B37 1992   261.8   C92-094791-3

LIBRARY OF CONGRESS CONTROL NUMBER: 2006927546

Cover design: Bill Douglas at The Bang

Canada Council
for the Arts

Conseil des Arts
du Canada

ONTARIO ARTS COUNCIL
CONSEIL DES ARTS DE L'ONTARIO

*We acknowledge for their financial support of our publishing program
the Canada Council for the Arts, the Ontario Arts Council, and the Government of Canada
through the Book Publishing Industry Development Program (BPIDP).*

Printed and bound in Canada

Contents

COMPASSION *and* SOLIDARITY

1. The Solidarity Movement in the Church

IN THE RECENT DEBATES OVER THE CANADIAN refugee policy the Christian churches were vocal in their defense of compassion and common sense. We learned from the mass media that organizations representing churches, synagogues, labour, and human right groups had become the defenders of refugees and advocates of a more generous public policy. They tried to calm the near-hysterical reactions that swept certain sectors of the population. Have the churches always stood up for the poor? Have the churches always been in solidarity with the victims of society?

In these five lectures I wish to speak of a new movement in the Christian churches that creates a startling link between religious faith and concern for others. What has taken place in the Christian religion is an outburst of compassion. I wish to dedicate these lectures to the memory of Bishop Adolph Proulx of Hull-Gatineau, Quebec, the compassionate and courageous champion of social justice, whose sudden death in the summer of 1987 deprived the Catholic Church of one of its most ardent and most influential activists.

In the first lecture I shall describe this faith-and-justice movement in some detail. The movement began among the few, it involved a minority of Christians, and, surprisingly, it has since been endorsed by the church authorities. This is true of all the major churches, Anglican, Protestant, and Roman Catholic. Since I am a theologian in the Roman Catholic Church, it is from developments in this tradition that I shall illustrate the meaning and power of the new movement.

In the second lecture I shall analyze the resistance to the new movement within the churches. Certain conflicts in the Catholic Church deserve attention, not least because they have a certain impact on society. In the third lecture I shall describe what this movement looks like in Canada. In particular, I shall analyze the radical social teaching of the Canadian Catholic bishops. In the fourth lecture I shall try to express the spiritual content of the new movement. It would be quite wrong to think that the new commitment to social justice affects only the ethics and the practice of Christians. I wish to show that it also affects their prayer, their perception of God, their spiritual life. In the final lecture I shall show that the social conflict over material things is actually, at the deepest level, a struggle over values.

In this first lecture, then, I wish to tell the remarkable story of how the explosion of compassion and solidarity took place in the Roman Catholic Church. It occurred, as I mentioned above, in all the churches. It happened especially in 1948, when the World Council of Churches, which has its headquarters in Geneva, was established. Yet the development in the Roman Catholic Church is so remarkable because this Church is known to be doctrinally conservative, committed to the ancient creeds, and defensive in regard to its own historical tradition.

The Catholic story must be told in two phases. The first one began in the early sixties with the Second Vatican Council, the full assembly of Catholic bishops convoked by Pope John XXIII. It was held in Rome from 1962 to 1965. A general council of this kind is an extraordinary event in the Catholic Church. The last one, the First Vatican Council, took place over a hundred years ago. The purpose of Vatican II was to permit the Catholic Church to find a creative response to the challenge of the modern world. Pope John said that he wanted to open the windows of the Church to let light and air come in. He wanted the Church to engage in self-criticism. He wanted the bishops of the Council to listen to the reform movements in the Catholic Church. And he wanted them to learn from the renewal efforts of the other Christian churches. At the Vatican Council, the Catholic Church discovered a new sense of solidarity with other religious communities and in fact with the whole of the human family.

It is no exaggeration to say that in the past, the solidarity of Christians was confined to Christians. In her official liturgy, magnificent though it was, the Catholic Church prayed only for the Christian people, not for outsiders, not for humanity. The one exception was the liturgy of Good Friday, when the Church prayed for the conversion of all outsiders to the Catholic faith.

To illustrate the new sense of solidarity, let me mention first the positive approach taken by the

Council to the ecumenical movement. This movement, created by Protestant and Anglican Christians earlier in the century, aimed at enhancing the unity of faith and action among the Christian churches. The Catholic Church had refused to participate in the ecumenical movement. At Vatican II, the Church modified its position. For the first time the Catholic Church recognized the other Christians as brothers and sisters in Christ, as co-heirs of the Gospel. The Council recognized other Christian churches as churches in the true theological sense, as believing communities used by the Holy Spirit as agents of grace and salvation. At the Council the Catholic Church committed itself to take part in the ecumenical movement.

I had the good fortune to be deeply involved in this effort of Vatican II. Pope John XXIII had appointed me as theological expert at the Secretariat for Christian Unity under the chairmanship of Cardinal Bea. One of the tasks of the Secretariat was to promote the spirit of ecumenism at the Council. We were allowed to invite Protestant, Anglican, and Orthodox observers. We engaged in dialogue with them and communicated their recommendations to the Council. More than that, the Secretariat submitted a draft proposal for a decree on ecumenism. The bishops were at first very cautious in regard to the new approach to other Christians and their churches, but the conciliar debate touched them and they changed their mind. To witness this spiritual transformation taking place in the Catholic Church was one of the most moving and exciting experiences of my life.

It is easy to document the impact of Vatican II on the relations between Catholics and Protestants in

Canada. Here the churches have learned to cooperate. While they differ in regard to certain points of doctrine, they stand for the same social values and adopt common positions on matters of social justice. Before John Paul II visited Canada in 1984, the Canadian churches published a joint letter addressed to all their members, in which they welcomed the Pope as a witness to the Gospel. I know of no other country where this happened.

In Canada, theological education has to a large extent become ecumenical. Catholics and Protestants read one another's biblical studies and theological writings; they use one another's textbooks. In some schools, for instance in the Toronto School of Theology, Protestant and Catholic seminaries and faculties cooperate in providing theological education for their students. Similar efforts at theological cooperation are found all over Canada and in the United States.

Of even greater importance is that on the social day-to-day level, Christians have overcome the estrangement of the past. They have learned to trust one another. Spiritual solidarity has come to transcend the confessional boundaries.

Of worldwide historical importance is the change in the Catholic Church's attitude toward the Jewish people and Jewish religion. The Vatican Council was willing to listen to the theological position worked out by critical Catholics who took with utmost seriousness the Holocaust, the mass murder of the Jews during World War Two. After the war, critical Christians, including Catholics and Protestants, created a movement in the churches to review the attitude toward the Jews. These Christians believed that the anti-Jewish rhetoric contained in the Church's teaching had created a paranoid, anti-Jewish public culture, a culture which made it possible for Hitler to make the Jews the scapegoat of Germany's and the world's ills.

What was this anti-Jewish rhetoric of the Church? Passages in the New Testament claim that by their refusal to accept Jesus, the Jewish people have excluded themselves from the divine covenant: Israel is no longer God's people. The Church is now the new people of God. In subsequent centuries this teaching was further amplified. The Jews were presented as betrayers of Christ, as unfaithful, as devoid of spiritual gifts, as cursed and punished by God. Over the centuries this preaching created contempt for Jewish religion in the Christian nations. After the War, the critical Christians argued that this teaching of contempt, and the anti-Jewish cultural mood produced by it, explain why there was so little resistance to Hitler's racist anti-Semitism, even though racism was at odds with Christian teaching. These critical Christians now called the Church to repentance.

Pope John XXIII called upon the Council to review the Church's attitude to the Jews and Jewish religion. After much research and many theological debates, Vatican II promulgated a statement on the Church's approach to the Jews that reversed the inherited position. Relying on St. Paul's statement in the New Testament that God never repents of the gifts given, Vatican II recognized that the Jews remained God's first-chosen people. The Church acknowledged its own Jewish roots. Jesus was a Jew; so was Mary, his mother; and so were the twelve apostles. It is wrong and inadmissible to blame the Jewish people as a whole for whatever the group of leaders did to Jesus during the time of his persecution. The conciliar declaration demanded that all formulations expressing contempt for Jews and their religion be removed from catechisms and books of religion. The Council recognized that Jews and Christians share a common spiritual patrimony. Christians acknowledge the spiritual substance of Jewish religion. What this means is that God continues to speak in the worship of the synagogue. The Council defined the relations of Catholics to their Jewish neighbours in terms of friendship, dialogue, and cooperation.

This conciliar teaching represented an extraordinary development. Many of us working at the Council at the time were grateful to God that we belonged to a Church that could change its mind.

Vatican II also honoured the religious pluralism of the global society. Again, this was new and startling. The Council clarified the Church's relation to the other world religions, especially to Islam, Hinduism, and Buddhism. For the first time the Catholic Church was willing to recognize something of God in these ancient religious traditions. All religious believers deserve respect. Catholics are called upon to engage in interreligious dialogue and find new forms of cooperation, especially in the fight against discrimination and the struggle for social justice.

A special conciliar document, entitled "The Church in the Modern World," expressed in an unprecedented way the Church's solidarity with the entire human family. Here is the opening sentence: "The joys and the hopes, the griefs and the anxieties of men and women of this age, especially of those who are poor or in any way afflicted, these too are the joys and hopes, the griefs and anxieties of the followers of Christ." In this document the Church defined itself as sent into society as friend and servant. It is the Church for others. Its task is to bear the burden with other people, to struggle with others for greater justice, and to strengthen the bonds that unite people, despite differences in religion, culture, and racial origin, and in doing so to become conformed to its Master who came to serve, not to be served.

It is no wonder that some conservative Catholics were unhappy with the new teaching of Vatican II. They feared that the Church had become excessively preoccupied with worldly issues and the relationship to outsiders. The true task of the Church, they said, is to proclaim God's glory. They felt the Church's concern had become too horizontal, that it should be more vertical.

The answer to these misgivings is that the Vatican Council did make important statements about God. Implicit in the call for universal solidarity is the affirmation that God is graciously present in the whole of humanity. Wherever people struggle with the important issues of truth and justice, they are not left to their own limited resources, but are assisted by a voice, not of their own making, that addresses and empowers them. The Vatican Council affirms that God's grace is not confined to the Christian Church but extends to the whole of the human family. All people, wherever they may be, the Council proclaims, are touched by the Spirit and enabled, in a manner known only to God, to participate in the redemption made visible in Jesus Christ.

Many Christians find this teaching startling. Yet Catholic theology over the last twenty years has greatly emphasized the universality of God's redemptive grace. This is not a new doctrine. It was taught by important theologians in the early centuries, especially in Alexandria; it was also taught by Thomas Aquinas and other medieval theologians. But it has moved to the center of attention only in our day. There are several reasons for this. One of them is undoubtedly the extended dialogue with Jews and members of other religions. Christians have become convinced that God spoke to their partners in dialogue. Cooperating with others in the struggle for justice has also convinced Christians that God is at work in people, be they religious or secular, who stand against oppression in solidarity with the poor and the powerless. Christians of our day have begun to realize the destructive historical consequences of the Church's traditional exclusiveness. Because the Church saw itself as the only place on earth where God's grace was available, it sanctioned the colonial exploits of European empires as a divinely given opportunity for its missionary work. Because of its narrow view of God's grace, the Church was unable to extend its solidarity to outsiders.

In the light of these new insights, Christians reread the Scriptures and find in them many hints that wherever people loved and sought justice, God was at work in their hearts. In the presence of Noah, God made a covenant with the whole of humanity. In John's Gospel we read that God's Word addresses every human being who comes into this world. Christians have become convinced that their God offers light and grace to people everywhere, enabling them to practice the love of neighbour. They have been especially moved by many stories from prisons, concentration camps, and countries ruled by dictators or foreign powers. These stories tell that here some people experienced within themselves a richness and an urgency to extend their help to those who were endangered, even if it meant endangering their own survival. Important Christian theologians -- Henri de Lubac in France, Karl Rahner in Germany -- came to the conclusion that the God revealed in Jesus and proclaimed by the Church was graciously operative in the entire human family.

All of this was incorporated in the teaching of Vatican II. Revealed in Christ is God's merciful presence to the whole of humanity. "Since Jesus died for all people and since all have the same divine vocation, we must hold that the Holy Spirit in a manner known only to God offers to every person the possibility of sharing in the event of redemption."

This is a startling message. In the past, Catholic theologians tended to distinguish the realm of the Church as "the supernatural order," defined by divine redemption, and the realm of the world as "the natural order," defined by divine creation and human sin. At one time, the theological distinction between the supernatural and the natural justified the Church's separation from the world. We then thought that the bond uniting Christians was "supernatural," produced by sharing in redemption, while the bond between Christians and non-Christians was of a purely worldly kind: it was simply "natural." Church-related activities of Christians were then regarded as belonging to the higher order, while their secular activities -- for instance, social and political involvement -- were seen as belonging to the natural order.

The Vatican Council transformed this theological perspective. The locus of God's redemption is not simply the Church but human history itself. God is present among us. God is the hidden presence that makes humanity possible.

To this point I have been speaking of the first phase of the transformation experienced by the Catholic Church in the past twenty-five years. This first phase was sparked by the Vatican Council. We now turn to the second phase of our story, ushered in by the world-shaking experience of the Latin American Church. From one point of view this second phase prolonged the spirit of Vatican II; but from another it was an independent start, to some extent critical of what went before. This second phase introduced the demand for liberation into the Church's teaching.

In the sixties and seventies the Latin American continent was in a turmoil. So were other regions of the Third World. The widespread unrest was described by Pope John Paul II as "the emergence on the political scene of peoples who, after centuries of subjection, were demanding their rightful place among the nations and in international decision making."

In the fifties, the developed nations, especially the

United States, ostensibly wanted to help Latin American countries to escape from their poverty. To do this, they encouraged the investment of northern capital in the south. They hoped that this would stimulate industrialization, create wealth, and provide jobs for the people. Yet in the sixties and seventies, Latin Americans discovered that this capitalist development, dependent on the United States, did not help them at all, because the northern owners of capital set up the new industrial developments so as to increase their own profit. Instead of producing foods and goods needed by the people, they produced commodities that would get a high price on the world market. Instead of using a simple technology that would provide employment for many workers, the new industries started with expensive, sophisticated technology that would require few workers. And often these workers were to be so skilled that they had to be imported from the industrialized north. The new industries, sponsored by northern capital, created a small class of managers and submanagers, people well paid by northern standards, who soon became a political force in their countries, defending the status quo and the power of northern capital.

Vast numbers of Latin Americans came to believe that the so-called help extended to them by the United States, Canada, and other developed countries only increased their economic and political dependency. It widened the gap between the few who were well off and the great majority who were pushed more deeply into poverty. What these Latin Americans demanded was independence from the international economic system with its center in the north. They wanted to develop a more self-reliant economy that would produce the foods and the goods needed by the people that would make use of simple, labour-intensive technology, that would offer employment to the masses. They called this liberation.

Liberation movements were organized all over Latin America and in other parts of the Third World. Among them were many Christians. In Latin America, Catholics committed to social justice formed small base communities; in these they helped one another in difficult times; they prayed together, read the Bible together; they involved themselves in joint social action -- getting clean water for their community, organizing village councils, protesting against oppressive practices. Some even gave their lives in this struggle.

In these base communities, "liberation" did not remain a purely secular concept. With their more secularly oriented neighbours, these Christians worked for their country's independence from world capitalism and toward the creation of a self-reliant economy. Yet for these Christians this struggle had religious meaning. They believed that the God of the Bible was on their side: God was on the side of the poor and oppressed. They attached great importance to the biblical story of Exodus, the liberation of the Israelites from oppression in the land of bondage. They believed that God's covenant with the people in the desert meant "never again Egypt," never again subservience to empire, never again oppression. They discovered in the Hebrew prophets that in situations of exploitation, God took the side of the exploited. God demanded justice. Even the worship of God was null and void unless people were dedicated to social justice.

Reading the New Testament, these Christians discovered that the preaching of Jesus was continuous with the Hebrew prophets. He called the poor blessed and castigated the rich and powerful. He called the poor blessed, not because misery was a good thing, but because he believed a radical transformation was about to take place: the coming of God's reign. The poor would inherit the land. These Christians recognized that Jesus was a threat to the established order. Like many Latin Americans who challenge the established order, he had been tortured and executed. Yet when God raised him from the dead, God vindicated all the victims of history.

You notice that the concept of liberation here still refers to the secular, historical process of overcoming oppression; yet this process, when looked upon with the eyes of faith, reveals itself as part of a wider and deeper transformation, grounded in God's redeeming presence, affecting all aspects of human life, spiritual and material.

The Christian communities of which I speak were often joined by priests. Some of them were trained theologians. They decided to collect and systematize the understanding of the Gospel that emerged in these communities. The resulting literature was called "liberation theology." The main points of liberation theology have been accepted by the Latin American bishops and have had an enormous impact on the Church's official teaching in North America and at the Vatican.

To clear up a frequent misunderstanding, I want to

explain that the base communities -- and following them, liberation theology -- do not look upon Jesus as a political leader. They do not regard the Gospel as a political message. The New Testament gives no encouragement for such an interpretation. With all Christians, liberation theology recognizes that Jesus was a religious leader. His message was in the first place a religious message. It had to do with God's presence, with God's love, with God's will for humanity, with God's approaching reign. The Gospel proclaimed God's judgment on human sin and God's promise of new life. Jesus preached salvation. According to the New Testament, this salvation was not purely spiritual and other-worldly. It had transformative power; it promised to make people new. It changed not only their spirits but their lives.

What was new and startling in the Latin American reading of the Gospel was that the passage from sin to new life, promised in Scripture, involved not only personal but also social transformation. In other words, the Christian Gospel has a political thrust. The religious message of Jesus has ethical and political implications. It condemns injustice and calls for a social order that reflects God's will for humanity. The Gospel is a subversive message.

The reading of the Gospel from the perspective of the poor and oppressed was so convincing that it influenced the Church's official teaching. The World Synod of Bishops, held at Rome in 1971, declared that "the salvation which Jesus Christ has brought includes the liberation of people from oppression." "Includes" is here the important word. Salvation is seen here as a broad, transforming divine movement, ultimately identical with God's gracious presence in history, that includes, as one dimension, the liberation of the oppressed and the reconstruction of society.

Who brought this radical message to the 1971 World Synod of Bishops? The Latin American hierarchy. Already in the sixties, the base communities and their liberation theologies had considerable impact on their own continent. When these bishops gathered at the now-famous Medellín Conference, held in 1968 at Medellín, Colombia, they produced an important document -- one that was to have great influence in Latin America and the entire Catholic Church. Certain chapters of the Medellín Document contain the principal elements of liberation theology. These chapters accept the analysis of Latin American poverty and dependency, which I have described; they endorse the struggle for economic and political liberation; they recognize that this liberation is part of the wider redemptive process promised in the Scriptures; and they accept that the personal decision to follow Jesus Christ in Latin America entails a commitment to liberation.

These Christians in Latin America, including their bishops, looked at the world from the underside, from the perspective of the powerless. They found themselves caught in the margin of a system of economic and political power, the center of which was far away in the north. They were frightened by what the future would bring them.

From their point of view, Vatican II had looked upon the modern world too optimistically. The important bishops and the influential theologians at that Council had all been from the successful Western European countries. They had assimilated, consciously or unconsciously, the concerns and aspirations of the middle class to which they belonged -- the "haves" as opposed to the "have nots." The Council's urgent call for dialogue and cooperation presupposed universal good will. But what if people are captured in structures of domination that are upheld and defended by those who derive benefits from this injustice? Here, it would seem, dialogue must give way to conflict. There are historical circumstances where revolution is justified.

The explosion of solidarity in the Catholic Church, then, had two phases. The Vatican Council was the great ecclesiastical event that revealed to Catholics all over the world that the Church was in motion. The Holy Spirit guaranteed that transformation was possible in the Church. Through the Council, Catholics discovered that they were coresponsible for their society. They saw themselves as sent to serve the world. This strongly affected Latin American Catholics. Yet as these men and women embarked upon their own service to the world, they followed a new perspective, not formulated by Vatican II, the perspective from below, which I have called the second phase. In this historical context, compassion and solidarity acquired a new meaning.

In this move the Catholic Church joined a development that also took place in the other Christian churches. First there was ecumenical generosity, openness to the world religions, and the support of people's human rights; and then, largely through the impact of Third World churches, there was the radical commitment to look upon the world from the view point of the poor and oppressed.

The new perspective from below has received a technical name in ecclesiastical literature. The Latin American bishops' conference meeting at Puebla, Mexico, called it "the preferential option for the poor." They produced a whole chapter to explore its meaning. Let me offer a precise definition. The option has two dimensions. The first one has to do with knowledge and the second with action.

The option is first of all a perspective for seeing the world. The option commits us to read society from the perspective of its victims. Usually we look upon society, or any social text, from the perspective of our friends and associates. This seems natural to us. We discuss what happens in society with the people close to us. If we happen to belong to a privileged class, we tend to interpret the world from this perspective. What the option for the poor asks of middle-class people is to abandon their own class perspective and read society from below, through the eyes of the people at the bottom and in the margin.

This option was made by many Latin American Christians, including their bishops. They looked at the continent through the eyes of the victims, who in Latin America constitute the great majority. They studied their society in the light of its contradictions. This option, prompted by faith in Jesus Christ, is the soul of liberation theology.

But the option for the poor has a second, an activist, dimension. It includes solidarity with the poor and their struggle for justice. It calls for action and public witness. What is presupposed here is that the poor -- the great majority in Latin America -- are to be the agents of their own liberation. Their struggle for justice will liberate Latin American society. All who love justice, therefore, of whatever class, must support the poor in their struggle for liberation. The Church itself, the Puebla Document declared, must be in solidarity with this struggle.

The preferential option is the startling message from the Latin American Church. It offers a profound challenge to the Church in the developed world, in Europe and North America. What is remarkable is that certain groups of Christians in these parts, along with their ecclesiastical leaders, have responded positively to this challenge. They have endorsed the option. They have been willing to look at their own society from the perspective of the victims and publicly express solidarity with their struggle for justice. Theological movements equivalent to Latin American liberation theology have emerged in many countries, including Canada and the United States.

The preferential option for the poor is a radical position that is often opposed in the Church and in society. When the Canadian bishops started to apply this option to their understanding of the Canadian situation, they were severely criticized by people accustomed to defend the status quo. The preferential option is still controversial in the Catholic Church, even though it has been endorsed in important ecclesiastical documents.

A little incident occurred in the summer of 1987 at the funeral service of Bishop Adolphe Proulx that revealed the controversial nature of the preferential option. The sermon was given by Bishop Bernard Hubert, president of the Canadian Bishops' Conference. In words that deeply moved the audience he praised Bishop Proulx as a compassionate and courageous churchman committed to the preferential option for the poor. Adolphe Proulx, though a gentle person, always spoke up, sometimes even in provocative ways, in support of workers and other groups who were made to bear the heavy burden of injustice. Bishop Hubert expressed the hope that Bishop Proulx's pastoral orientation would be followed by the entire Catholic Church in Canada.

When after the funeral Mass the diplomatic representative of the Vatican to the Canadian government, Bishop Angelo Palmas, gave a short address, it became clear that he was not comfortable with the preferential option for the poor. He expressed his discomfort indirectly. He praised Bishop Proulx for having practiced what he called "the preferential love of the poor." The Vatican bishop offered the audience an explanation of what precisely this expression meant. Christians are called to a love that is universal. All people, rich and poor, are entitled to our love, but those whose need is the greatest, namely the poor, have a preferential claim on our love. We must help them first.

There is no doubt that this is a sound Christian principle. But this "preferential love" is not at all equivalent to the preferential option for the poor, which -- as we saw -- implied a socio-critical perspective guiding both the perception of society and the active engagement to transform it.

Such is the explosion of solidarity in the Church that it shakes the foundation and divides people of good will.

2. Opposition to the Solidarity Movement

IN ALL THE CHRISTIAN CHURCHES there is a movement of greater openness to the world religions. The churches have declared themselves in solidarity with the whole human family. In the Catholic Church it was the Second Vatican Council in the sixties that introduced this new spirit. Since that time the new movement has experienced a second, more radical, phase. For many contemporary Christians, faith in Jesus has come to generate a yearning for social justice -- not just in name only. We all say we believe in social justice, but these Christians have been acting on their belief, putting themselves on the line. Their radical spirit is well expressed in a sentence written by the Canadian Catholic bishops in one of their pastoral messages: "As Christians, we are called to follow Jesus by identifying with the victims of injustice, by analysing the dominant attitudes and structures that cause human suffering, and by supporting the poor and oppressed in their struggle to transform society."

This is truly a stunning declaration. And everything it stands for has evoked strong resistance in the churches. I am going to analyze this opposition, but this is no easy task since the new movement suffers from an internal tension between its liberal and its radical phase. Many Catholics rejoiced in the new openness of the Second Vatican Council, the new ecumenical spirit, the new respect for personal conscience, and the humanistic interpretation of the Christian message. But now they are puzzled and even disturbed by the more recent social teaching that places world hunger and other forms of economic oppression at the center of attention. They are troubled by the ethical critique of contemporary capitalism put forth by John Paul II and the Canadian bishops.

The openness of Vatican II allowed Catholics to participate in contemporary culture and feel at home in its humanistic currents. The new social teaching, on the other hand, is quite critical of middle-class culture because it tends to reconcile us to the unjust distribution of wealth and power in the world.

The reaction of secular society has been similar. The North American public, including the mass media, were delighted by the liberalization and the spirit of dialogue introduced by the Second Vatican Council, yet the same public has been puzzled by the socio-critical stance taken by the recent church documents. In Canada the press has often been angry with the Catholic bishops for adopting a viewpoint critical of the present economic system. Political leaders in the Conservative and Liberal parties, too, have been severely critical of the bishops' social teaching. As politicians they know they will not lose Catholic votes over this. They are fully aware that the Church's new social philosophy is supported by only a minority of Catholics.

As for the other Christian churches, they, too, suffer from the same internal tensions. There are conservative Christians who cling to the religion as they have inherited it; there are liberal Christians who are open to the world and to other religions and have a humanistic understanding of the Christian message. And then there are radical Christians for whom faith implies support for the poor and who find themselves at odds with modern society.

At present we are witnesses of a new cultural trend sometimes called neo-conservative. This trend emphasizes personal ambition and free enterprise, tries to reconcile us to social inequality, and gives us a good conscience when we are exclusively concerned with promoting ourselves. This neo-conservative spirit generates a special hostility to the social justice movement in the Christian churches. It is almost as if Canadian society and the churches have moved further apart at this time. A good example in Canada is the contrasting reaction to Native land claims. For the last decade or so, the Canadian churches have given moral, legal, and concrete financial support to Native organizations in their struggle with the government.

There are, of course, significant sectors of Canadian society that have responded to the social activism of the Christian churches with enthusiasm. Labour organizations have praised it; so have the unemployed; so obviously have the Native Peoples, and members of the New Democratic Party.

I wish to deal now with the opposition to the new movement in the Catholic Church. Many of my observations also apply to the opposition in the other Christian churches. Let us begin with the Christians sometimes called conservative. Many good Catholic and Protestant people oppose the new openness of their respective Churches and the new sense of universal solidarity because they love their religion in the form in which they have inherited it. They have had their important religious experiences in the more traditional framework. Some conservative Catholics feel that the changes made by Vatican II were due to the pressure exerted by a well-educated minority in the Church, whom the bishops were unable to resist. Prior to the Council, these Catholics defended their faith when they were challenged by Protestant opinion and the hostility of secular culture. After the Council, they were not immediately ready to turn around and embrace ecumenism and dialogue with the world. Such religious conservatism is usually accompanied by social conservatism. These Catholics tend to be opposed to social change.

I feel very strongly that conservative Catholics, and correspondingly, conservative Protestants, deserve great sympathy. They fear social change because in their own experience such change has always been imposed on them from a distance, without their having anything to say about it. In the past they were always reassured that at least their religion was inviolable and their own. Even the strong -- even the bishops and the Pope -- had no power over religion but, as every one else did, had to follow and obey it. So these Christians oppose the new movement in the Church for truly religious reasons, not because they have high stakes in the existing social order or want to protect the privileges they might have. It comes down to what their sense of religion is. And the only thing that can move these Christians is new religious experience.

The religious and social conservatism of such good people has, alas, always lent itself to exploitation by the powerful. Political figures whose conservatism is based on their wish to protect the power and privilege of the few easily find support among them -- as do bishops and popes whose conservatism is based on their wish to defend the existing order or protect their own power.

However, as I have already said, the great majority of Catholics in North America are pleased with the new openness of Vatican II. They appreciate the more humanistic understanding of the Gospel and the new openness to the world. They are liberals; they think in terms of personal growth and personal freedoms. They do not fully understand the Church's more recent radical message. They imagine therefore that now the bishops are accusing them of not doing enough for the poor, of not giving enough money or of not extending themselves as they should. They do not understand that the new radical teaching offers a structural critique of society as an entity. What is being questioned is not individual virtue but the whole economic setup that regulates production and distribution and the impact of this system on culture and public values.

These Catholics are puzzled. In English Canada and the United States the Church has, over several generations, tried to teach Catholics, many of whom were recent immigrants, to seek education, apply themselves, work hard, improve their economic condition, and make it in the competitive industrial society. Catholics have done this faithfully, all the while retaining their spiritual values and bringing up their children in the Catholic faith. Now, after they have joined the middle class and the mainstream of North American society, they learn that the Church has shifted its orientation and raises serious questions about the values it has affirmed.

These people are often good and generous Catholics. But like the rest of us in North America, they do not have a very developed political consciousness. They do not recognize the ideological dimension implicit in the accepted view of contemporary society. They look upon society as the social framework that offers individuals the freedom to compete and pursue their chosen purposes, yet they do not see this as an individualistic political ideology undermining social solidarity. This ideology prevents people from discovering that society is a social project, for which they are together responsible. That is why they find it difficult to grasp the new social teaching.

In my opinion the same puzzlement is experienced by a great many Protestant Christians. They don't quite understand the radical statements made by their own Church leaders.

Still, many of these Christians have their eyes opened through new personal experiences, through contacts with immigrants from the Third World, or through political involvement to protect the underprivileged in Canada.

A third group of Catholics do not take the Church's new teaching seriously because in their eyes the Church lacks credibility. Its inflexible position on women persuades them that the progressive statements of bishops and popes are merely words. It is true that until now the Church's official teaching has not acknowledged the subjugation of women as a justice issue. The Church's solidarity with the powerless does not seem to imply solidarity with women in their struggle against patriarchy. While many pastoral statements made by Canadian and American bishops have adopted a feminist perspective, the Pope and the Vatican still defend the traditional subordination of women.

These Catholics feel that the official Church has lost its credibility also by its inflexible stand on sexual matters. In the late sixties Pope Paul VI created a large study commission, made up of lay people, doctors, psychologists, theologians, and bishops, to study the question of birth control. The great majority of this commission published a report that recognized the morality of "artifical" birth control for couples who made responsible decisions about the number of children they wanted to have. Nevertheless, Paul VI decided to uphold the traditional ban on contraception. Catholics found it difficult to explain why their Church came to ethical conclusions that were so different from the corresponding positions taken by the Anglican and Protestant churches, especially since the Bible had so little to say on the matter. And they argued that the reason for this difference was the fact that the decision-making body in the Catholic Church is exclusively made up of unmarried men, reflecting a one-sided perspective.

Significantly, among the Catholics for whom the Church has lost credibility, one might also mention many Quebeckers who are still angry with the Church for the unenlightened political and economic policies it promoted in the past, prior to the Quiet Revolution of the sixties. Despite certain notable exceptions -- for instance, Archbishop Charbonneau during the Asbestos Strike in the fifties -- the Quebec bishops of those earlier years appeared to bless the Duplessis government, including its anti-labour policies and its anti-human rights positions. Today many Quebec Catholic with long memories wish the Church would remain silent on issues of social and political ethics.

For all these Catholics the teaching of the Church on moral issues and matters of justice has lost its credibility. That is why they don't get excited about the new faith-and-justice movement. Some of these Catholics are friends of mine. I have often argued with them. In my opinion the explosion of solidarity in the Catholic Church, and in all the Christian churches, expressed in the practical struggle for peace and justice, is a turning point, an event possibly of world historical importance. It represents nothing less than a reversal of Christian history. If the churches in cooperation with the other world religions *reject* in their traditions what has fostered inequality and strife, and *retrieve* those elements of their traditions that call for justice, peace, and participation, there is hope for the earthly future of humanity. For this reason I argue with my friends that even if the Catholic Church is at this time still inflexible when it comes to women and issues of sexuality, there is reason to be hopeful.

I have left till the last the Catholics who oppose the new movement in the Church because of vested interest in the status quo. They accuse the radicals of being naïve, romantic, and even dangerous because their rhetoric allegedly supports socialism, or even Marxism. These Catholics usually have high stakes in the present system and its distribution of power and wealth. They regard it as the source of stability in the world, and so they fear that the Church's recent critical teaching will undermine the order in society. These are the people who relied on the Church to bless the powers of this world; now they are disappointed that the Church seems to have withdrawn its approval. They hope that the new social teaching will remain purely rhetorical and that in its day-to-day action the Church will continue to be the friend of the powerful.

The political philosophy defended by reactionary Catholics is actually opposed to the entire tradition of Catholic social teaching, not just to the more radical position. Still, in the U.S.A. these Catholics have created an organized, well-financed opposition to refute the social teaching of their own bishops. They have published pastoral letters and sent them out to the parishes. There is no reason to be surprised by this. The class conflicts in society over wealth, power, and prestige translate themselves into tensions within the religious communities, in this case the Christian Church.

In a recent column in The Toronto *Globe and Mail* Mr. Conrad Black, the well-known businessman and publisher, accused the Canadian bishops of having become "trendy, biased, misleading, and reckless." He claims they have fallen into grave error, encouraging dangerous tendencies among the Canadian people. The column is not written in a spirit of dialogue. The author makes no attempt to understand recent Church teaching and then to formulate his critical response. Instead, he distorts this teaching from the outset and responds mainly with invectives.

What Mr. Conrad Black completely overlooks is that the identification with the poor is not an invention of the Canadian Catholic bishops but represents an international movement in the Catholic Church and in the other Christian churches. I want to reply to Mr. Black by quoting an extrememly provocative statement made by Pope John Paul II on his Canadian tour in 1984. He told us that we must evaluate our society in accordance with these ethical principles: "The needs of the poor must take priority over the desires of the rich, the rights of workers over the maximization of profits, the preservation of the environment over uncontrolled industrial expansion, and production to meet social needs over the production for military purposes."

The new social thinking has been endorsed by the Catholic Church. This is also true of the World Council of Churches and many Anglican and Protestant churches. Outstanding in the Catholic Church are the social justice statements made by the episcopal conferences of Latin America, of Canada, and of the United States, supported by several important Vatican pronouncements, not least among them John Paul II's 1981 encyclical on labour.

At the same time, many bishops in these countries and many Vatican churchmen are uncomfortable with this radical position. Some of them try to give a purely moralistic interpretation of the identification with the poor, as if it simply asked people and church organizations to be more generous to the poor.

Let me try to analyze the conflict within the Church hierarchy. Many of the bishops personally share the religious convictions I have described above that prevent ordinary Catholics from joining the new movement. There are "conservative" bishops deeply attached to the inherited form of Catholicism who feel ill at ease with the recent changes. They are suspicious of ecumenism and dialogue and uncomfortable with the social radicalism implicit in the new social teaching. But there are also "liberal" bishops pleased with the openness of Vatican II who are puzzled by the new emphasis on preferential solidarity. They are afraid that the preoccupation with social issues will distract the Church from the more urgent pastoral work among the great majority of the people. And then there are undoubtedly also "reactionary" bishops, consciously or unconsciously allied to the powerful and their economic interests, who are unhappy with the direction contemporary Church teaching has taken. While they may not speak against the new teaching in public, they will give the impression to their friends that much of its rhetoric is simply figures of speech.

But you cannot study the behaviour of large organizations such as Christian churches by confining attention to the personal convictions of the staff officers. To study large organizations you have to make an institutional analysis. Allow me, then, to deal with one institutional conflict in particular that plays an important role in large organizations such as the Christian churches.

I would argue that in all organizations two operative logics are at work. The first one I will call the "logic of mission." It is defined by the end and purpose for the sake of which the organization was created. Universities, broadcasting corporations, churches, governments -- all are institutions created to serve a particular purpose or mission. And the other logic at work in an organization is the "logic of maintenance," defined by the need of the organization to maintain itself. An organization must have a well-trained staff, adequate housing facilities, a sound financial basis; it must remain publicly credibile. If an institution paid no attention to the logic of maintenance, it would disappear very quickly.

In all large organizations then, including the churches, conflicts often occur between the logic of mission and the logic of maintenance. Anyone who has attended board meetings of large institutions is fully aware of this. Certain staff members make proposals -- sometimes bold proposals -- that try to make the organization more effective in the exercise of its task and, if possible, increase its outreach. In reply to these proposals, other staff members -- those more directly concerned with maintenance -- will explain the difficulties the proposed activities will create: there is not enough money; the staff is already overburdened; the supporters of the organization will be offended; many people, possibly the most influential in society, will not like it. Our own experience confirms that conflicts between the logic of mission and the logic of maintenance are inevitable. On the whole, a lively conflict between the two logics is beneficial for the organization.

However, sociologists have observed that in all large organization the logic of maintenance tends to become dominant and overshadow the logic of mission. Institutions easily become preoccupied with maintaining themselves, often to the neglect of the end and purpose for the sake of which they were originally set up. It is true, of course, that it would be fatal for any organization to be unconcerned about its financial situation, its staff, and its institutional needs. Yet the greater temptation is to allow the concern for maintenance to become the primary preoccupation of the organization. If this trend is not resisted, the organization is likely to become self-contradictory: it will no longer serve the purpose for which it exists and it will eventually lose public credibility and in this way prepare its own demise.

Before applying this sociological reflection to explain the opposition among certain Church leaders to the new movement in the Catholic Church, let me say a few words about another institutional conflict operative in all large organizations between the center and the outlying regions. We are accustomed to this conflict from the political debates in Canada between the centralizers who want to strengthen the power of the federal government and the advocates of greater provincial independence. The same conflict also takes place in the Roman Catholic Church.

From the Renaissance on into the twentieth century, the centralization of power in the Roman papacy was the dominant and almost unchallenged institutional trend. When the Catholic Church was confined to Europe, this system seemed to be functional. The Catholic regions outside of Europe tended to be looked upon as colonial developments subject to European ecclesiastical control. Yet over the last decades the non-European churches have become impatient. Following the secular trend toward independence, the churches in the Americas, Africa, and Asia have demanded a certain responsible decentralization of power. The Vatican Council in the early sixties, bringing together the bishops from all over the world, seriously challenged the age-old centralization of decision-making in the papacy and its administration. Since Vatican II, the various national hierarchies in the Church have been constituted as episcopal conferences and as such, collectively, have made many pastoral decisions as teachers and planners that were formerly reserved to the initiative of the Vatican. The new movement in the Church, analyzed in these lectures, favours responsible decentralization in the Church. A greater sense of collective self-responsibility allowed the Latin American bishops to define the preferential option for the poor and charter a new pastoral orientation for their churches. The American and the Canadian episcopal conferences have also taken a more independent, creative approach in their pastoral policies and their social teaching. These decentralizing movements in the non-European churches do not deny the supreme central power invested in the papacy. What they ask for is simply a shift of balance, a new equilibrium that grants greater independence to the regional churches.

The centralizers in the Catholic Church oppose the new movement of which I speak because it strengthens the demand for greater regional independence. The course of action pursued by John Paul II and his curia at the present time aims at weakening the decentralizing trend introduced by Vatican II and resetting the balance in favour of the papal government.

Recently, opposition to the new movement of solidarity has become quite vocal at the Vatican, with Cardinal Ratzinger at the head leading it. Josef Ratzinger is an important German theologian, who was ordained a bishop and later, under Pope John Paul II, became the head of a Vatican organization formally called "the Holy Office." He fulfills a certain watchdog function for the Church's central administration. Why should he be uncomfortable with the Church's new openness to the world and the option for the poor? His opposition can be explained as an excessive application of the logic of maintenance. He represents the churchmen who feel that the new movement in the Church weakens the collective identity of Catholics, undermines their spirit of obedience, and threatens the Church's material security. What has happened is that the new openness initiated by Vatican II can obscure the boundary between Church and world. Catholics who enjoy ecumenical solidarity with Protestants, have sympathy for the world religions, and cooperate with their fellow citizens, whether they be religious or secular, may lose a sense of their collective identity. That which is distinctive in their tradition, especially the link to the hierarchy, may begin to appear insignificant compared to the spiritual gifts which they share with others. Catholics may then not be able to hand on to their children a strong sense of identification with the Church, which makes difficult institutional demands on them. The children of such

Catholics may feel that they are part of an ecumenical movement, in solidarity with all people of good will, especially those who have been pushed to the margin.

According to the logic of maintenance, such a development would be dangerous for the Catholic Church because it would weaken the ecclesiastical organization. Catholics would make themselves more independent of the ecclesiastical authority and pay less attention to the Church's teaching authority. Pope and bishops would find their power reduced. What this objection overlooks is that built into the Christian message is an unresolvable conflict, a source of great creativity, between identification with the household of faith and universal solidarity.

Not only that, but the emphasis on participation and coresponsibility in the Church's recent social teaching could make Catholics impatient with the nondemocratic style of the ecclesiastical government. According to it, people are called to be "subjects" or "responsible agents" of their society and of any organization to which they belong. So participation today is regarded as a human right. But if this right is emphasized in the religious education of Catholics, they are likely to demand coresponsibility and power-sharing in the Church.

I am convinced that the papal-episcopal system we have inherited is in itself no obstacle to consultation and participation and that what coresponsibility demands is simply a new style of decision-making in the Church.

There is a further point to be made. The fact that the Church has sided with the poor in several ecclesiastical documents could easily offend the worldly powers, on which the Church willy-nilly depends in its day-to-day existence. At one time the state expected the Church to bless the existing order. The dominant classes, while not religious themselves, were often favourably disposed toward the Church because it blessed the established order and only called for modest reforms. But now the Church has adopted a critical stance. I have already mentioned the hostility of the powerful. What happens if the Church loses the support, however indirect, of the established order? Can the Church maintain its institutional life in such a precarious situation? To answer this question we have to listen to the teaching of Jesus.

Let me turn to safer grounds. I want to give an example of the opposition mounted by Cardinal Ratzinger at the Vatican against the new solidarity movement in the Church. At the Vatican Council, after a long debate, the Catholic Church became willing to honour the other Christian churches as true churches. It became necessary, therefore, to relativize to a certain extent the inherited self-understanding of the Catholic Church as the only true Church of Christ. A phrase in a conciliar document which said that the Church of Christ "is" the Catholic Church was eventually replaced by another which said that the Church of Christ "subsists in" the Catholic Church. Avoiding simple identification, the Council left room for the subsistence of other churches in the one Church of Christ. All churches in one way or another participate in the one Church of Christ. The ecumenical implications of this modification were enormous.

In a recent speech Cardinal Ratzinger proposed the theory that the Vatican Council had not modified the self-understanding of the Catholic Church at all, that the meaning of the words "subsists in" was identical with the previous "is" and that therefore, by implication, the other Christian churches were not Churches in the proper theological sense. Fortunately, Cardinal Ratzinger's theory was refuted, not only by Catholic theologians, but also in a recent speech given by Cardinal Willebrands, formerly the president of the Vatican Secretariat for Christian Unity. His public support was greatly appreciated.

In a recent statement Cardinal Ratzinger also tried to discourage Jewish-Christian dialogue. He insisted that in conversation with Jews, Catholics must not hide that Jesus is the messiah of Israel in whom the ancient promises have been fulfilled. This remark evokes the traditional opposition between the victorious church and the blinded synagogue. By contrast, the Second Vatican Council clearly recognized the evil historical consequences of this and similar anti-Jewish images in the history of the West. What the Council emphasized, therefore, was that despite their different readings of Scripture, Christians and Jews share a common spiritual heritage. The Church no longer desires the conversion of the Jews; instead, it invites them to dialogue and cooperation, jointly to cultivate the common heritage.

In 1984, Cardinal Ratzinger published an instruction that warned Catholics of the dangers associated with liberation theology, in particular its "insufficiently critical use of Marxism." The subsequent debate in the Catholic Church led to a second instruction signed by

Cardinal Ratzinger in 1986 which fully recognized the emancipatory thrust of the Gospel and the close link between salvation and liberation. This was followed by a letter of John Paul II to the Brazilian bishops, clearly affirming the value and importance of liberation theology.

On the whole, I think, a lively conflict between the two operational logics -- the logic of mission and the logic of maintenance -- is a healthy phenomenon in an institution. It exercises an important progressive function if it helps to promote the Church's mission -- without undermining its institutional base. I conclude, therefore, that the conflicts at present taking place in the Christian churches are not signs that the new movement for peace and justice will come to an end. The explosion of solidarity in the churches is bound to give rise to strains and tensions. But because the scriptural and moral authority of the new movement is so overwhelming, it will survive these conflicts, and flourish in the future.

3. The New Social Gospel in Canada

Almost every day we read in the newspapers that the churches have made a critical statement in regard to an important social issue. Earlier this year, along with the synagogues, they called for a more generous legislation in regard to refugees. The churches have expressed their solidarity with the Native Peoples and supported their land claims. And they have published statements on unemployment, Northern development, world hunger, the farm crisis, immigration, arms production, and free trade. Canadians have been puzzled by this new concern.

At the same time, the newspapers report almost every day that the churches in other countries, especially in Third World countries, also exercise their social responsibility. They stand in solidarity with the victims of society. What has happened?

In Canada this new faith-and-justice movement took off at the end of the sixties, occurring in an ecumenical context. The churches were ready to work together. They created several interchurch committees with the mandate to study what social justice meant in various sectors of Canadian life. The churches did this as a response to the aspirations of a network of socially concerned Christians all over Canada. Some of these groups represented people suffering injustice in this country, for instance Native Peoples or the unemployed. Other groups were in solidarity with struggles in the Third World and tried to influence Canadian public policy. The new movement, therefore, began at the grass roots. It has received the support of the church leaders. Still, it represents a minority in the churches.

For the Protestant and Anglican churches, this recent development represents the return of the Social Gospel. The Social Gospel was a faith-and-justice movement that began in the late nineteenth century. It offered a wider interpretation of the Christian message: God demanded justice in society. In Canada the Social Gospel exerted political influence in the twenties and in the thirties during the dark years of the Depression. It was involved in the creation of the radical political party, the Cooperative Commonwealth Federation (CCF). Not surprisingly, the faith-and-justice movement at that time did not receive the blessing of the church leaders. The return of the Social Gospel in our day is based on a sounder theology and a better grasp of the social sciences. And this time around it is endorsed by the ecclesiastical leadership. It is, moreover, part of a worldwide movement.

As for the Roman Catholic Church, the recent development represents a startling evolution of its traditional social teaching. The Canadian bishops were willing to listen to the victims of society, to learn from the prophetic tradition of the Bible, and to enter into dialogue with Canadian political scientists who analyzed the ills of society. The bishops were accompanied in this by the other Canadian churches. They were inspired by the radical position adopted by many Third World churches and supported by John Paul II's recent encyclicals.

The Canadian Catholic bishops published many pastoral messages and statements that tried to clarify what the radical commitment to social justice means in Canadian society. Since the early seventies they have produced a body of literature that contains the beginning of a Canadian critical social theory. In this lecture I shall present some of the dominant themes of this new teaching.

Let me start with the Labour Day message of 1976. Here the Canadian bishops offer a brief statement of what the new Social Gospel means in Canada. The pastoral document is a gem. It is in my opinion the best expression we have of a Canadian liberation theology.

It begins by recognizing the historical situation: "We live in a world that oppresses at least half of the human race and this scandal threatens to get worse." This is a strong statement by the bishops. While we in Canada have our own suffering, we belong nonetheless to the small sector of the world that claims the larger part of available resources. "The present social and economic order fails to meet the human needs of the majority of people." It widens the gap between the rich and the poor and leaves the control of resources in the hands of an elite. The peoples of the Third World in particular clamour for the creation of a new economic order, based on a more just distribution of wealth and power.

What is the summons of the Gospel in this situation? As disciples of Christ we must act out of dedication to justice. One sentence in particular reveals how deeply the bishops feel the urgency of their faith in God: "We stand in the biblical tradition of the prophets of Israel where to know God is to seek justice for the disinherited, the poor and the oppressed. The same Spirit of God that came upon the prophets filled Jesus of Nazareth. With the power of that Spirit he announced that he was the message of the prophets come true -- 'the good news to the poor' and 'liberty to the oppressed' [Luke 4: 18-19]."

The Labour Day message continues: "For Christians the struggle for justice is not an optional activity. It is integral to bringing the gospel to the world."

I have quoted the bishops verbatim to reveal the spiritual foundation of their radical social teaching. In their eyes, the commitment to social justice is not purely secular; it has profound religious meaning. In compassion and solidarity, people find God.

It is the Church's task to evaluate society in accordance with the values revealed in the Gospel. The bishops realize that this is new and radical. It is a call for conversion, addressed to all members of the Church. "Unfortunately," they admit, "those who are committed to this Christian way of life are presently a minority in the life of the Catholic community." They call this minority "significant" because it summons the whole Church to greater fidelity. The bishops actually defend this minority against the criticism levelled against them -- "particularly," as they say, "by the affluent and powerful sectors of the community."

What does the bishops' call to conversion mean in practical terms? How should Christians think and act in a society such as ours? The Labour Day message proposes several guidelines.

The guidelines call upon us to reread the Bible, to hear in it God's call to justice. In the past, we tended to hear in the Gospel only the call to love our neighbours individually, to be generous and to help them as much as possible. A rereading of the Bible in our day has revealed a new definition of neighbour: "We want to build a society in which all members are treated as neighbours, as people deserving respect." Today, almsgiving is no longer enough. Love of neighbour calls for social justice, for a transformation of society, so that the victims will be delivered from their crushing burdens. In our day the love of neighbour generates a passion for justice.

The guidelines ask us to listen to the victims of society. We cannot come to know Canadian society if we only talk to our friends. Even our newspapers tend to see social issues from the perspective of the middle class. Mainstream culture tries to make invisible the sins of society and allow the victims to disappear from our consciousness. Many of us never meet the poor, the unemployed, and the people who live in daily fear of insecurity. The dominant culture tries to give the middle class a good conscience. What the bishops dare to tell us is that to arrive at an honest evaluation of our society, we must first listen to the people who suffer injustice, we must look at history from below. And then we can speak out against injustice.

Many people find this difficult. A certain modesty and a desire to be kind and well behaved often makes it difficult for church-oriented Christians to participate in public demonstrations. To be seen on protest marches is embarrassing to them. Respectable people don't do this. The bishops ask us to reconsider our feelings here. Faith and solidarity call for public protest.

Yet it is also necessary to analyze the causes of social injustice. Why are the Native Peoples oppressed? Why is there massive unemployment? The bishops claim that the causes of these fateful historical developments can be analyzed scientifically. At one time, before the advent of modern medicine, people thought that illnesses happened out of the blue: they did not know then that the cause of disease could be analyzed scientifically. Similarly, many people believe that poverty and other collective misfortunes just happen. However, dialogue with social science is convincing ever-wider sectors of the population that the causes of unjust social conditions can be analyzed scientifically. The Canadian bishops, following here a famous remark of Pope Paul VI, urge Catholics to engage in social analysis. And then we must act.

Christians are asked to participate with other citizens in political action to remove the causes of oppression from society and transform the social order.

Clearly, the Canadian bishops fully endorse what the Latin American bishops have called the preferential option for the poor. This option comprises a double commitment: to look at society from the perspective of its victims and to express solidarity with them in public action.

Allow me to mention here that this bold option for the poor has been endorsed by Pope John Paul II, in his 1981 encyclical on labour. Applying this option to the developed nations of East and West, communist and capitalist, the Pope provocatively called for "the solidarity of labour supported by the solidarity with labour."

In the guidelines of the Canadian Labour Day message, Christians are also asked to help the poor and needy. The new, politically responsible understanding of Christian discipleship must not make us forget the continuing need for almsgiving and acts of compassion. They remain essential. While foodbanks, for instance, do not deal with the causes of unemployment and hunger, they are nonetheless necessary in the present situation. Christians should support both the struggle to transform society and the effort to offer temporary assistance to its victims. The struggle for justice must always be accompanied by compassion.

In my opinion, the brief Labour Day message of 1976 is a cogent statement of a Canadian liberation theology. The statement affirms that the redemption brought by Jesus Christ and preached by the Church includes the liberation of people from the conditions of oppression. The statement unfolds the meaning of this Christian message in the concrete conditions of Canadian society.

In subsequent pastoral messages -- especially in the famous statement of 1983, called "Ethical Reflections on the Economic Crisis" -- the bishops have applied their own critical principles to come to a better understanding of the contradictions of Canadian society. They worked together with the other churches and were attentive to the debate among Canadian social and political scientists, and from this produced elements of a critical social analysis. They laid the foundation for an original social theory.

In the second part of this lecture I wish to present the critical analysis of Canadian society found in the pastoral messages of the Catholic bishops. I must warn listeners that the social analysis and the recommendations are quite radical. To put their cards on the table, the bishops revealed the methodology they employed in preparing their pastoral messages. The pertinent text is so important that I shall quote from it, in a slightly abbreviated form.

"Our pastoral methodology involves a number of steps: (a) to be present with and listen to the experiences of the poor, the marginalized, the oppressed in our society, (b) to develop a critical analysis of the economic, political, and social structures that cause human suffering, (c) to make judgements in the light of the Gospel principles concerning social values and priorities, (d) to stimulate creative thought and action regarding alternative models for social and economic development, and (e) to act in solidarity with popular groups in their struggles to transform society."

Let me jump right into the social analysis offered by the bishops. They focus on the injustice and inequality produced by the economic institutions. They present what is called a structural analysis. They look at the changing face of capitalism in Canada and relate it to the wider crisis of the world economy.

This approach is new in Catholic social teaching. In the past, Church teaching tended to put primary emphasis on the moral dimension. The Church denounced hard-heartedness, greed, and selfishness.

It called for an ethical conversion on the part of all, and it held out the hope that love of justice and greater generosity could reform the existing economic institutions.

More recently, especially since the Pope's encyclical on labour, church documents begin their analysis of social evil by focussing first on the economic infrastructure. Only after that do they call for new values. Economic analysis here precedes value analysis.

Some people might ask what do theologians know about economics. In the last two decades or so, theologians have been studying economic developments from an ethical point of view. Nowadays church seminaries hire faculty in this area to instruct the students.

To begin with a structural analysis is important, the Canadian bishops say: otherwise we are tempted to blame innocent people for unemployment and economic decline. Some may claim, for instance, that workers are lazy and do bad work. Others suggest that immigrants or women take away their jobs. Society has an unfortunate tendency to blame the victims.

We cannot understand the social deterioration taking place in Canada and in the world unless we analyze the changes in the structure of capital. The bishops outline five trends: the concentration of capital, its centralization, its internationalization, the increasing foreign ownership of the industries, and the switch to computer technology. I want to look at these five trends.

By the concentration of capital the bishops refer to the trend to move financial and commercial institutions into the metropolitan areas. This is done to increase efficiency and profits. Yet this trend leads to regional disparity. Visible examples of this concentration are the new head-office banking towers in Toronto, the giant structures built like temples, gold-tinted and decorated, that shape the city's skyline and symbolize the new economic gods. Many regions in Canada now find themselves deserted by companies and offices that had brought economic life to their communities.

By the centralization of capital the bishops refer to the trend of large corporations to increase their profitability by buying out and taking over smaller and medium-sized companies. Because these takeovers are regularly reported in the newspapers, they are perhaps the most visible sign of where the economy is going. Concentration of capital means concentration of power. An ever-shrinking elite is involved in making the important decisions in regard to Canada's economic life. So great can the power of these giant corporations become that they are able to force government to serve their interests.

By the internationalization of capital the bishops mean the recent trend to increase the profits of industries by relocating them in parts of the world where labour is cheap, where safety regulations are minimal, and where governments forbid the unionization of workers. This trend has led to the deindustrialization of many regions in Canada. Companies that have for a generation or two drawn upon the labour and the cooperation of entire communities suddenly decide to leave them.

By increasing foreign ownership the bishops refer to the trend of foreign -- especially American --

companies to increase their holdings of certain industries in Canada. Several of our industries have become branch plants of American companies, and the decisions regarding their operation and development are made by directors in a foreign country who have no reason to be concerned about Canadian workers. It is not surprising that in a recent Church document the bishops express their fear that the free trade agreement with the United States will make Canadian workers even more vulnerable.

And finally the bishops point to the social impact of the new technology. Industries are becoming more capital-intensive. This means that more money will be spent on the technological equipment and less on wages. And fewer people will be employed.

It is this changing structure of capital, the bishops conclude, that is responsible for growing unemployment and the widening of the gap between the rich and the poor in Canada. This trend is universal. Capitalism is entering a new phase, one that will lead to the suffering of the masses. The bishops offer an interpretation of what is happening that is identical to the analysis proposed by the Pope.

After World War Two, forty-three years ago, capitalism entered a relatively benign phase. Capitalists realized that they needed the support of society. Under the pressure of labour unions and progressive political parties, they entered into an unwritten contract with society to provide full employment, support welfare legislation, and respect labour unions. But this unwritten contract is now coming apart at the seams. Unemployment has become massive, welfare legislation is under attack, and efforts are being made to discredit and even destroy labour organizations. In the opinion of John Paul II, the new phase of capitalism, unless stopped by political forces, will create enormous suffering in world society.

This analysis of society is unsettling. Most commentators on the Pope's teaching pretend that he did not say such things. But the Canadian bishops have been severely criticized for it. They have been called idealists, Marxists, or woolly socialists. One argument repeated many times is that the bishops are against profit. For them, it is said, profit is a dirty word. But this argument misinterprets their teaching. Everyone knows that a business or a company must pay for itself and make some profit. An economic system that does not make a profit cannot serve the needs of the people. What the bishops criticize is the maximization of profit. They argue that if an industry maximizes profit and technical efficiency, workers will be looked upon simply as material factors in the productive process, along with the raw materials and the machinery. Workers will become "objects" of the productive process, while they ought to be and are destined to be "subjects", that is, responsible agents, of production.

The bishops evaluate the present economic situation in ethical terms. They have produced an ethical critique of capitalism. Ethics is the Church's concern. The principal moral argument used in this context is the dignity of human beings. Because of their dignity, people are meant to be subjects or responsible agents of their society. Workers are meant to be subjects of the productive process. The dignity of workers is such that they are entitled to share in the ownership of what they produce and in the decisions regarding the organization of labour.

According to John Paul II, if workers are excluded from this coresponsibility, they live in a state of alienation. They feel pushed to the margin. Many of us know what this means. Workers are thus alienated in the two antagonistic systems, in communism and in capitalism. In communism the power over the product of labour is in the hands of the state bureaucracy. In capitalism this power is in the hands of the owners, or the directors plus managers. The social imagination which the Christian tradition brings to the great economic debate calls for increased participation of workers in the industries and greater democratic control of the economic institutions.

It is impossible to do justice to the emerging Catholic social theory in a single lecture. The bishops' teaching raises many questions that deserve careful answers. The reason that this teaching sounds so radical to us is that we are surrounded by cultural symbols that legitimate the existing order. To question capitalism seems daring in our culture, almost dangerous. While the dominant culture encourages us to raise critical questions in regard to many values, including religion, it regards it as improper to challenge the existing economic system. It is almost as if capitalism were something sacred. One of the great services the bishops have performed for us through their teaching is that they have demythologized the taboos of the dominant culture and invited us to engage fearlessly in ethical reflection on the economic trends of our times.

The bishops have looked at Canada from the

perspective of the disadvantaged. Some people have objected to such a negative approach to Canadian society. Don't the bishops love their country? Does not the love of country demand that we adopt a more positive perspective and show gratitude for the benefits we receive? I reply to this objection by recalling a sentence, uttered under quite different circumstances, by Paul Tillich, the great German-born Protestant theologian. He, too, was criticized for being too negative. He replied that to love your country well means to long for it to be just.

Exactly what policies do the bishops recommend? And who is to be the agent, the motive force, to introduce these changes in society? We have time only for brief answers to these important questions.

According to their pastoral methodology, the bishops make proposals to stretch people's imagination and give rise to a public debate open to alternative models of economic and social developments. They feel that we are caught in a cultural trap. Our imagination has been so impoverished that we think the only choice available to society is between capitalism and communism. What we need are alternative models.

What the bishops propose is based both on old Catholic teaching and on more recent developments. They recommend two policy orientations in tension with one another. On the one hand, we need more democratically controlled economic planning around the supply of the essential human needs. This includes planning around the production of food, housing, and jobs. This involves policies that protect our farmers and policies in regard to Third World countries that take into consideration their needs as well. This centralizing trend in public policy is to be balanced by a decentralizing trend. The bishops propose a greater decentralization of capital. Is the existence of the giant corporations, which control a substantial sector of the economy, good for society? What would a decentralization of capital look like? It would involve a diversification of ownership. Anti-trust legislation could break up the giant concerns, and new forms of public and cooperative ownership could be encouraged. One can easily imagine a society in which privately owned companies represent one sector of the economy, the other being made up of community-owned and worker-owned industrial and commercial enterprises. The bishops' proposals here follow the labour encyclical of John Paul II.

At this time, the only countries that increase productivity -- Japan, Sweden, and some other European countries -- are societies where workers are admitted to responsible participation and where it has therefore become possible for management, workers, and government to cooperate.

The new social imagination proposed by the bishops is made of two contrasting trends, one centralizing -- more democratic overall planning -- and the other decentralizing -- more democratic forms of ownership. The tension between these two trends is to guarantee the freedom of persons in society. The emphasis on more central planning recalls the socialist tradition, while the emphasis on the diversification of ownership balances this and invokes the cooperative movement. These are home-grown Canadian ideas: the wheat pools of the prairies, the credit unions of Quebec, the farmers' and fishermen's cooperatives in the Maritimes. While the bishops base this social imagination on Catholic values, they are keenly aware that the same sort of imagination is generated by other Christians, and by secular groups in society.

The bishops' proposals are controversial. Are they practical and will they steer the country toward greater social justice? Or will they lead to economic decline, as some of their adversaries insist? The bishops join here the great economic debate that engages the Western world at this time. Economists themselves are in disagreement. Economics departments at universities are communities in conflict. Some economists defend the more recent monetary trend as the solution; others advocate a return to Keynesian principles; and a third group, while by no means unanimous, advocates somewhat more radical surgery for the present economic order. It is my impression that it is with this third group, or at least with some of its members, that the Catholic bishops have the greatest affinity.

Why do economists disagree among themselves? Do they not all regard ecomonics as an empirical science? They all follow the scientific method. They all try to demonstrate their economic theories with empirical evidence. How then can we explain this profound disagreement among them? The cause for the difference among economists lies in the value assumptions implicit in their approach to economic science. What is the aim of an economic system? What primary issue attracts an economist's attention? How do economists conceive of the human being in their investigations? What role do they assign to cultural values in the process of production? While economics

-- like medicine -- is indeed an empirical science, it is a scientific enterprise divided by a conflict over values.

In 1982 the MacDonald Commission, presenting itself as non-partisan, invited groups and agencies in this country to submit briefs that would analyze the economic ills and recommend policies that could overcome them. Among these submissions were those of the Christian churches. Once published, the MacDonald Report turned out to reflect only the recommendations of the economically powerful groups. Whereupon two political economists, Daniel Drache and Duncan Cameron, decided to publish a book, called *The Other MacDonald Report*, that made available to the public the submissions of "the popular sector" to which no attention had been paid. This popular sector included trade unions, women's groups, social agencies, and organizations representing Native Peoples, farmers, and the disadvantaged. It also included the churches. What is remarkable is the unaniminity among these various groups.

This is how Drache and Cameron describe the consensus: "The popular sector groups contradict the urgings of business that government reduce its role in the economy and give free reign to 'market forces.' The economy must serve human well-being rather than corporate balance sheets, the popular sector says, and for this end a fundamental break with the conventional value system of policy-making is the only means available. They reject a view of economics that separates ends from means and that is based on having people adjust, accommodate and lower their expectations to the short-term profit considerations of business."

Many Canadian political economists have come forward and declared that the bishops' proposals make good economic sense. What these scholars have in common, and what they share with the bishops, is that they analyze Canadian society from the perspective of the people at the bottom and in the margin.

This remark leads us to the next question: Who is to introduce these changes in Canadian society? Who is to be the agent of social transformation? The older Catholic social teaching made proposals for the reform of society that depended on the good will and generosity of all concerned. All citizens, poor, rich, and in between, were called to an ethical conversion. The more recent Catholic social teaching rejects this idealistic approach. Society will only change if those who are disfavoured in it get organized and exert political pressure. John Paul II called this principle "the solidarity of the workers and with the workers."

In line with this new orientation, the Canadian bishops recommend the creation of a solidarity movement made up of the various groups and sectors which suffer under the present economic order, and supported by all citizens who love justice. The Church itself, according to them, should be in solidarity with such a movement.

This recommendation differs from what Marxists call "class struggle." In ideological Marxism, "class" is defined in purely economic terms. Each class is here seen as following its own collective economic self-interest. By contrast, the solidarity movement of which the bishops speak -- and to which *The Other*

MacDonald Report alludes -- is an ethical achievement. Each group is obviously concerned with improving its material situation, whether the group is made up of workers, of women, of Native Peoples, of the unemployed, or the handicapped. Yet to create a joint movement each group must respect and make room for the aims of the others. To create a coalition that can exercise pressure in society and become an agent of social change, each group must be willing to modify and adjust its own aim. A solidarity movement of this kind is an ethical achievement. It serves the material betterment of all in a context defined by principles of justice. That is why people in more favoured circumstances who love justice are called upon to support the movement.

This is the bold teaching of the Canadian bishops. This is the Social Gospel in Canada.

4. God as Comforter and Liberator

IN THESE LECTURES I HAVE BEEN DISCUSSING a new movement in the churches, one that binds Christian faith to the yearning for social justice. I have been maintaining that what has taken place is an explosion of compassion and solidarity, and this new movement has important spiritual implications. It has generated new principles of social ethics and summoned forth the Church's involvement in the struggle for justice. But in addition, it has also created new forms of prayer and produced new theological reflections on the biblical God.

Let me begin this fourth lecture with the hopeful message, formulated by modern theology and endorsed by the Second Vatican Council in 1965, that God is graciously present in the whole of humanity. People wrestling with issues of truth and justice are not simply left to their own limited resources: they are deeply touched by a light and a strength not of their own making: the sign of God's gracious presence.

According to this message, the redemption of Jesus Christ is an *inclusive* event. It touches the whole of the human family. Here is one of Vatican II's famous sentences: "Since Christ died for all, and since the ultimate vocation of humans is one and divine, we ought to believe that the Holy Spirit, in a manner known only to God, offers to every human being the possibility of being associated with Christ's redemption."

This is the theology on the basis of which Vatican II opened the Church to the world, fostered dialogue with the world religions, and urged Catholics to cooperate with others, be they religious or secular, to build a more humane world. Cooperating with these others, Catholics would encounter God, God incarnate in humanity.

Not only were their actions affected; the emerging theology affected Catholics in their perception of God and hence their mode of prayer. According to this theology, God is graciously present in human history, which means that God may not be thought of as the divine ruler, the heavenly father, the sky divinity, who governs the world from above. For many Christians this has been the dominant image of God. God looked down from a heavenly realm on humans and their history below.

Yet if God is mercifully present in human history as enlightenment and empowerment of people and their communities, we will have to abandon the split-level imagination with which we were at one time comfortable. We will want to think of God in nondualistic terms. God is Life with a capital L. God is Truth and Love with capital letters. God is the unconditional source of all truth and all love in this universe. God is the matrix out of which we move forward, the vector that directs our lives, and the horizon toward which we are called.

God is here not "over and above" but "in and through." Theologians call this God's immanence. Of course, God is at the same time transcendent. God is sovereign and unconditional origin. God is other. But divine otherness need not imply that God is far away, over and above, ruling the world from on high. God's otherness here rather specifies what we call the mode of divine immanence. God is graciously present in human history, but never imprisoned in it, never compelled by it, never exhausted by it. God is immanent but forever transcending. God is forever new and surprising. God present in history remains forever judge of the world, condemning it for its injustice, and forever redeemer of the world, enlightening and empowering people to build a more human society.

If God is a life-giving gracious presence rather than a superperson ruling from above, what does this mean for prayer? This is an important topic. For the moment let me just say a few words about it. If God is a presence in human life, then in prayer, listening is more important than speaking. We find ourselves addressed, challenged, judged, forgiven, and inwardly restored. Christians hold that they are being addressed by God in Scripture and liturgy: but once they have heard the divine summons there, they will also recognize the Word addressing them in their personal experiences and their historical situations. God speaks to us, not only in sacred space, but in the ordinary circumstances of every day. This at least is the confident message implicit in the theology of Vatican II and that of many other Christian churches. The secular is not as secular as it appears on the surface. Hidden in our encounters with other people and in historical events is a voice, not of our own making, that addresses us.

Prayer then is the quiet readiness to be spoken to, the longing to hear the voice. It is a listening that does not bracket personal experiences but takes them seriously. Personal experiences and our response to historical conditions are regarded not as distractions to be pushed aside but as the important events out of which we shall be addressed by the divine summons.

If prayer is listening -- and responding -- Christians do speak to God, but they do so because they have been addressed by God first. The ultimate response to God's voice is surrender. It is the heart of Christian prayer. Surrender stands behind all the words used in prayer and gives them their valid meaning. Surrender is also silent prayer.

The theology of the Second Vatican Council suggests that this surrender is easy. The optimistic strains in the documents of the Council persuade us that the primary truth about the world is God's presence in it. We listen into the world, rejoice in human self-exploration, and detect in it God's gracious call.

But this is not the whole story. Discipleship of Christ includes the preferential option for the poor and powerless. This is a term that has sprung into public consciousness since Latin American Christians have identified themselves with the poor on their continent. This starting point offers a perspective that is less sanguine about society focussing instead on social evil. It recognizes society as divided between "the powerful," who have arranged in their own favour the structures that distribute wealth and honour, and the "powerless," the victims, who constitute the great majority of the world's population.

From this point of view Christians in this movement believe that the God of the Bible is biased. God takes sides with the victims. Many Protestant theologians speak of "God's bias for the poor." God is the light and the strength of people in their struggle for justice.

What are the spiritual consequences of the option for the poor? What are its implications for prayer and for the doctrine of God? I wish to raise the spiritual question from the viewpoint of persons who, like myself, belong to a developed nation, to Canada, to a so-called successful country.

Among the poor in Latin America and other parts of the Third World, the faith-and-justice movement of the last twenty years has generated many new religious experiences, brought forth songs and poetry, and created a strong sense of hope and joy. These people feel that a *kairos*, a special moment, has arrived in their history, that they are about to free themselves from age-old subjugations. God graciously affirms their struggle.

But what I wish to focus on here is the dark side of the preferential option for the poor; that is to say, the side experienced by Christians culturally identified with the forces of oppression. This means, in effect, those of us in affluent nations.

In fact, the literature coming out of Latin America today records the crisis of faith experienced by Christians from the privileged classes as they enter into solidarity with the great majority. This entry is for them like a conversion, a transformation of consciousness.

They now see their Latin American society in a totally new light. They now realize that the reason they have been unable to see the truth about their society has been the blindness produced in them by the dominant culture. The culture in which they grew up and received their education has reconciled them to the existence of the poor masses as an inevitable fact of life. Their culture has exercised an ideological function: it has made them blind and deaf to the immense human suffering on their continent. The culture that distorted their perspective included religion.

A well-known Catholic activist in Brazil, called Frei Betto, tells us that after his conversion to the perspective of the poor, he was overwhelmed by the ideological distortion of the culture in which he grew up. Even the God in whom he believed became suspect. God and religion seemed to belong to the ideological symbols that had blinded him in regard to the endless suffering in his own country. The God of Catholicism and the promised divine salvation had been so heavenly, so otherworldly, that inequality among people appeared to him as a minor issue. Ultimately the rich and the poor, if they believed, would be saved for heaven.

Frei Betto tells us that after his conversion he no longer believed in the God whom he had previously accepted. He feared that he had become an atheist. In his anxiety and pain, he sought advice from an older brother in his religious order whom he trusted. The good man told him not to be afraid but to accept the silence and the loneliness -- and to keep waiting in the dark. Eventually God would speak again. And this God would then be in solidarity with the poor and the powerless.

The religious experience of *the oppressed* is that God is on their side. Society and the world may have discarded them, but God accepts them and empowers them. Alleluia! By contrast, the religious experience of *the more privileged* is profound outrage. They are overwhelmed by the sense that the suffering they see is against God's will and that it must and can be stopped. This religious experience demands that Christians extend their solidarity to the oppressed and join them in their struggle for justice.

And so Christians, like Frei Betto, are driven into spiritual darkness. In the language of the mystics, this dark side is called the *via negativa*, the way of negation. Historically, the mystics passed through the painful realization that everything said of God was untrue and therefore had to be negated. Every word used to designate God was of human size. Every word inevitably referred to the finite. Since God was infinite, every word that referred to the divine was therefore more untrue than true. God language must first be negated.

The preferential option for the poor gives the *via negativa* a wider sense, one not yet found in the classical mystical tradition. And it is not restricted to the Latin American experience. I wish to explore this dark side in reference to two different experiences, "the dread of ideological distortion" and "the breakdown of trust."

The important German Catholic theologian, Johann Baptist Metz, tells us that he grew up in a small Bavarian village fervently engaged in Catholic faith and practice. Everyone went to Mass on Sunday. Even during the week, before going to their work in the fields, the farmers and their families attended Mass. During the Second World War, when Metz was in his early teens, the Nazi government had a death camp built in the region, about fifty kilometres away from the village. The camp became a place of mass murder. Metz remembers that the existence of this camp was never mentioned in the village. Everybody somehow knew about the camp, but no one reacted to it. No one ever said a word about it. No reference to it was ever made in church. No prayers were offered for the victims. Daily Mass went on as if nothing had happened.

The memory of this experience has haunted the German theologian ever since. He has opted for solidarity with the victims. As a theologian he now asks himself the anguishing question: What was it in Catholic practice, in the steadfast piety, in the daily liturgy, that made the people mute and unable to react to the ongoing slaughter of human beings? He does not doubt for a moment that his fellow villagers were good people, faithful, generous, and sincere. He does not blame them. But he is driven to ask the question: Was there an ideological taint, implicit in the religion they had inherited, a distorting message, that made them react in such an inhuman way in the face of mass murder in their own neighbourhood? Was their religion an ideology, a myth, designed to make people subservient to, and uncritical of, those in authority, no matter what?

What I would define as the dread of ideological distortion has been the guide of Father Metz's entire theological work. He has braved the darkness, walked through the *via negativa*. And he has also developed a theological language that allows him to speak of God and the Good News in ways that express the divine solidarity with the oppressed. The German theologian has devised a provocative theological principle. "You cannot do theology with your back turned to Auschwitz." Only by facing the Holocaust in solidarity with the victim can Christians hope to articulate their faith in a manner free of ideological distortion.

Identifying with the poor has taught us that religion can be used to legitimate domination. Theologians have coined a new word for this. They call "sacralism" the use of religion to legitimate oppression. They hold that God is on the side of the victims and that the biblical message promises the lowly rescue from the death-dealing powers in history. They hold therefore that God's Word, uttered in Scripture and human experience, delivers religion from sacralism.

But as Christians face the ideological distortions carried forward in the Church's history, they experience dread, anguish, and fear. They will ask themselves whether the whole of their religion is not ideology, a myth designed to protect the white man's civilization and the privileges of the powerful. Is God just a cultural construction?

There are those Christians who simply remain in the *via negativa*. They never come out of it. Eventually they cease to believe. This happens to some Christian women who make the disturbing discovery that the biblical religion and the biblical God reflect the patriarchal structure of ancient society and hence bless and legitimate the supremacy of men. Some women have lost their faith over this. Other women, after the darkness, have come to believe that the biblical God, in solidarity with victims, is the ever-surprising transvaluator of values. God forever shakes the foundation. Christians may hope therefore that God acting among us will free the biblical message from its antifeminist bias.

What is required then is that Christians in solidarity with victims be willing to bear the dread of ideological distortion. Liberation theology tends to distrust philosophical tradition and the rational arguments for the existence of God, because such philosophy promises access to wisdom without commitment to those who suffer. Liberation theology is suspicious of a metaphysics that claims to demonstrate the existence of spirit without taking into account world hunger and other threats to humanity. There is access to wisdom only for those who open themselves to feeling or experiencing the plight of the oppressed. A theory that promises access to the truth, available -- without commitment -- to people on the sole condition that they be intelligent and can understand sophisticated arguments is likely to be an ideology. It pretends to offer wisdom without causing outrage over the death-dealing powers.

The metaphysics of the Bible proceeds from the Exodus story, in which God delivers the people of Israel from oppression in the land of bondage. For Christians, specifically, metaphysics also proceeds from the resurrection of Jesus, the innocent victim. In the vindication of Jesus, God has vindicated all the innocent victims of history.

The twentieth century has multiplied social evil on a

scale that transcends human imagination. For the people of the Western world, it is the Holocaust, the mass murder of the Jews in World War Two, that constitutes an event that interrupts and explodes all theories of human progress and all theologies of divine providence. The Holocaust points to other death-dealing modern fabrications of genocidal or near-genocidal proportions. On several continents the massive spread of hunger and misery, aided by an evil maldistribution of wealth and power, reduces people's life expectancy and increases infant mortality at an ever- increasing rate. Nations are dying. As Mahatma Ghandi once said, "Hunger is a form of violence" -- to which I would add: the dominant form of violence in today's world.

And then there is the nuclear threat. It was made real by the first dropping of the atomic bomb on Hiroshima and is amplified today in the conflict between the two competing empires of East and West, with its accompanying Cold War rhetoric, and the nuclear weapons race. Social philosophers have referred to these events as "the new darkness" of the twentieth century. Brought up in the optimistic culture left over and derived from the evolutionary imagination of the nineteenth century, and supported by the Western world's economic success in the twentieth century, we find it hard, if not impossible, to assimilate the idea of this new darkness. It disperses our dreams and it shatters our theories.

How do Western Christians react to this? Especially how do those Western Christians who made the option for the poor respond to these events? I have already mentioned their profound outrage. Such evil deeds have been produced by human processes and human planning, by institutional developments in which we have voluntarily or involuntarily participated. There is no doubt, we are a sinful world. While these Christians recognize the human responsibility for history, they cannot escape the tormenting questions: Is God not all-powerful? Why did God permit these events? Can God be trusted? Is it possible to pray after Auschwitz?

These questions continue to be asked by Jews and by Christians. There are many people who, face to face with "the new darkness," have had their faith in God totally shattered. We probably all have friends who are no longer believers. They may not call themselves atheists because that would give the impression that they want to make a theoretical affirmation. They have simply become secular, leaving the entire matter of faith behind.

Yet Jews and Christians who still think of themselves as religious must continue to ask the question whether it is possible to pray after Auschwitz. They experience not a theoretical but an existential doubt. They try to pray but find it impossible. They listen but there is no voice and no melody. Deep down they, too, no longer trust God.

Trust is the foundation of prayer. Trust is implicit in the beginning of prayer when we listen to God's message addressing us. And trust is intensified during prayer when we reply to God's Word in life-giving obedience. Surrender is the deepest dimension of prayer. Many people are called to sustain prayer with lamentations over the suffering of the world; others are called to sustain it with pleas for mercy and rescue. But eventually prayer is destined to become surrender. It is the unconditional Yes to God that gives the words and gestures of prayer their fullest meaning.

Christians enter fully into the *via negativa* when the new darkness robs them of their ability to surrender and hence to pray to God.

A Jewish religious thinker has said that Auschwitz has put an end to "untroubled theism." From now on, there is room only for a troubled theism. This is true, I think, at least for those of us in Western society. It seems to me that people lack religious sensitivity if they remain unchallenged by the new darkness and claim that their trust in God has remained unaffected.

In our times, anguish and doubt have become part of the dialectic of faith. It seems the more we believe that God is love, the more impossible it becomes to believe in God.

The Catholic theologian, Father Metz, whom I have mentioned several times, gave an important reply to the question whether prayer after Auschwitz is possible. It is possible to pray after Auschwitz, he said, because there were Jews at Auschwitz who went on praying.

Metz adapted here a statement made by the German philosopher Adorno who had declared, right after World War Two, that after the Holocaust it was no longer possible to write poetry. The Holocaust had definitively interrupted the imagination of beauty. Several years later, Adorno changed his mind. It is possible to write poetry after Auschwitz because some Jews in the death camps actually composed poetry. Many such poems have been found. The imagination of beauty survived even in the kingdom of horror.

From the memories of survivors and from documents hidden and saved, we know that people in the death camps prayed to God. Their trust was not shattered. Because of them, because of their witness, said Father Metz, it is possible to pray after Auschwitz.

In this context I wish to mention the witness of an extraordinary young woman, Etty Hillesum, a Dutch Jewess, arrested, imprisoned, and eventually killed in a death camp, whose diaries have only recently been published. In English her book is entitled *The Interrupted Life*. Her story is remarkable from many points of view. What impressed me especially was her spiritual transformation in the camp. She, an educated, secular person, found herself addressed by God. She was called into a life characterized by total solidarity with her suffering people and total surrender to the God intimately present to her. Her surrender to God and the repudiation of her own resentment were experienced by her as a form of social resistance to fascist domination. She was overwhelmed by God.

We have arrived at a paradox.

I have argued that the explosion of compassion and solidarity in the Catholic Church has taken place in two phases, in tension with one another. The first phase was the Church's new openness, initiated by Vatican II, and the second phase was the conversion of the Church to the option for the poor. Both phases have profound spiritual implications. This is what I have dealt with in this lecture. The new openness of the Church, I have tried to show, is based on a new perception of God's presence in history, on a nondualistic imagination about the divine, on a sense that God is graciously present, as enlightenment and strength, in people's struggle to become fully human.

By contrast, the preferential option for the poor made the ready trust in God's presence in history appear unrealistic. The preferential option causes outrage among people such as ourselves, born and living in the affluent West. The pleasant language of love, friendship, and cooperation can easily be taken for an ideology of the successful, disguising the historical conditions that cause suffering to the majority of humankind. Can we say that God is love to people who suffer oppression from political and economic structures, in which we, however unwittingly, are participants? Are we not taunting them by this sort of language? In a society marked by grave injustice, the love of neighbour transforms itself into a yearning for justice and an impulse to act so that the heavy burdens be lifted from the shoulders of the victims. In a sinful world, love calls for preferential solidarity. We are not in solidarity with Pharaoh and his supporters. Only when the historical conditions of justice have been created can solidarity become universal. Preferential solidarity is the first step toward the unfolding of a truly universal solidarity.

Please, do not misunderstand me. I do not recommend that we who belong to a privileged society, or a privileged sector of society, should feel guilty. Guilt feelings are appropriate for evil deeds we have personally committed. Our integration into the dominant structure of society is more fateful. The appropriate response is to mourn : mourn a world that allows racism, that engages in a nuclear arms race, and that consents to world hunger. The option for the poor,

I have tried to show, makes traditional God language problematic. Can one repeat the sentence that God is present in history while standing before a Nazi death camp or facing Third World peoples caught in hunger and misery? The option for the poor pushes Christians into what the mystics called the way of negation, the *via negativa*. We must first negate as untrue everything that is said of God. This has always been a painful path. The *via negativa* of the present, after Auschwitz and the new darkness, includes what I have called the dread of ideological distortion and the breakdown of trust. Both paths lead to sorrow, anxiety, and doubt.

We have reached the paradox of God's presence and God's absence. Throughout my discussion of the two dark paths, I have repeatedly hinted that the way of negation need not be the end. Because of the witnesses, because of Moses and the biblical prophets, because of Jesus who died and rose and who ushered in God's reign, and -- in our own time -- because of the clouds of witnesses under the rule of terror, Christians find themselves affirming again, despite the darkness, the God of life. They are now able to give a different meaning, a new and deeper meaning, to the contemporary spirituality of openness and to the claim that God is graciously present in history. Yet Christians find it difficult, if not impossible, to find words to express this difference. Because they have passed through the way of negation, the language of God's presence no longer presents a rosy picture of the world, nor fosters indifference to the suffering of the oppressed. In a deeper, unexpected, and ineffable way, the affirmation of God's presence is quite true. The mystics called this final step the *via eminentiae*, the way of expanded meaning.

In the twentieth-century world, the easy talk of God's universal grace remains unacceptable. It is the great temptation of middle-class people in developed countries to interpret the Gospel as a religious practice that enhances their lives in a spiritual way. They are sensitive to the God-given humanistic implications of the Christian message. The Gospel becomes for them too easily a source of joy. It makes them generous: they wish the whole world well without confronting the data of despair.

But the option for the poor invalidates this interpretation of the Christian message. If we look at history from below, we hear in the Christian message first of all God's judgment on the world. For people caught in oppression, the Gospel is first of all affirmation; but for people associated with the dominant culture -- such as we are -- the Gospel is judgment before it offers new life. It is only after we have mourned, after the way of negation, that the joyful language of God's gracious presence recovers its true and authentic meaning.

A church organization in Quebec, called l'Entraide Missionaire, holds a yearly congress in Montreal that deals with Third World oppression and the challenge it offers to the Church's mission. At the congress held in September 1987, we spent two days in sessions and workshops analyzing the structures of economic, political, and structural oppression. And we mourned. Yet at the eucharistic liturgy which closed the congress we were able to celebrate God's presence, renew our hope, and experience joy. These were the words of the final song: "La ténèbre n'est point ténèbre, devant toi la nuit comme le jour est lumière." In English: "Darkness is no

longer darkness, before you the night is like the day."
If this verse were sung by people who looked at the
bright side of life, the words would be a disguise for
the injustices and the suffering in the world. The verse
would be irresponsible poetry. But singing them after
the *via negativa* at the missionary congress, the words
had a different, new, and expanded meaning. They
meant that despite it all, and in the face of it all, even
though we see no immediate solution, we resist, and
in this resistance we are consoled by God's presence
and God's promise.

So the tension remains. In a privileged country like
Canada, the way of negation can never be totally left
behind. We never totally overcome the dread of
ideological distortion, nor the breakdown of trust.
Mourning and lamentation become a permanent
element in the worship of God. At the same time,
Canadians are greatly comforted by the hope and the
cheerfulness of so many Third World Christians in
their struggle for justice, despite the danger in which
they live. Canadians are helped again and again to pass
beyond the negative way to the recognition of God's
presence in their lives. When this happens -- and for
some this happens often -- the prayer of surrender is
possible. If they yearn for justice and question their
society, Canadians are not excluded from
contemplation and ecstasy.

5. Conflict Over Values

A NEW MOVEMENT IN THE CHURCHES has linked faith and the yearning for justice. An explosion of solidarity has taken place in which Christians interpret the biblical message as a divine summons to build a just and peaceful society. In many parts of the world the churches, or sectors of the churches, have involved themselves in public struggles for human rights and social justice. In Canada the Christian churches have taken strong positions on many social issues, speaking out on unemployment, on refugees and immigration, on Native Peoples, on cooperating with nuclear programs of the United States, and on many other issues. The Canadian Catholic bishops worked out a critical social theory that offers us an analysis of Canadian society and a new imagination for alternative models of economic and social development. Of course, in a democratic society, bold transformations are possible only if they are supported by a groundswell of public opinion. Bold institutional changes work only if they are accompanied by new cultural values.

The public wrestling for social justice must include both a political and a cultural dimension: political because it concerns the distribution of wealth and power in society and aims at transforming the social order, and cultural because it involves a conflict over values. This is how the churches see it. In the last analysis, the way in which we organize ourselves as a society reveals what we believe about human beings and their common destiny. So our self-organization as community has theological implications. In their pastoral letter on economic justice, published in 1986, the American Catholic bishops claimed that the socio-economic order "influences what people hope for themselves and their loved ones; it affects the way they act together in society; it influences their very faith in God."

That the struggle about the economy is political and cultural is not something new to students of sociology. An economic system produces the goods that satisfy people's material needs and desires, and in doing so also distributes power in society -- alas, unevenly. Why do people put up with a setup that serves a minority better than it does the majority? Because the power of government normally defends the inherited order. Yet the more powerful protector of the system is culture or, more correctly, mainstream culture. The state does not usually enforce the order of society against the will of the people. What happens rather is that mainstream culture creates in people certain values, norms, and expectations, which makes them accept the given system as a good thing. Culture legitimates the existing order.

That the dominant culture blesses and stabilizes the existing order is a theory accepted by sociologists from both the left and the right wing, from the Italian communist Antonio Gramsci to the conservative

American sociologists Talcott Parsons and Peter Berger, who regard society as an acceptable equilibrium that deserves support. But what precisely do these sociologists mean when they say that "culture" legitimates the social and economic order? The word "culture" here does not refer primarily to music, poetry, and works of art. Sociologists often call these "high culture." The word "culture" in this context refers to something more ordinary, to something that involves us every day. Culture refers to the set of values, symbols, laws, and institutions that express the vision and the ethos of a society and regulate how people treat one another.

For example, science and technology are part of our culture. They promote a certain rational way of thinking; they encourage certain virtues, such as no-nonsense efficiency; they make us dream of a universe fully controlled by us and discourage reliance on nonscientific ways of knowing; they persuade us to think of society in mechanistic terms and suggest that ethics and religion are at best purely private choices with no public validity. Science and technology produce a powerful cultural trend in Western society. We are all aware of it. It affects us whether we like it or not. At the same time there are also cultural forces resisting this trend.

For one thing, the churches stand against the mechanistic trend in modern society; so do the synagogues; so do the other world religions and secular traditions that also promote an ethical vision of society. Ethical values cannot be confined to the private sphere. Religious institutions make moral demands on society as a whole. They stand for a social order and a public life that respect the dignity of the human person, of all human persons. This is an ethical position that cannot be demonstrated by science nor assured by technology.

And the churches have always offered a critique of modern culture. We are accustomed to this. What is new today is that the Christian churches, responding to the social justice movement, have begun to critique contemporary culture from the perspective of the poor and oppressed. In this process the churches are discovering in how many ways the dominant culture blesses and legitimates the existing order, despite its many injustices. In Canada the Christian churches are in ecumenical conversation. They cooperate in particular in clarifying the demands of social justice for Canadian society. The Catholic bishops, supported by the other church leaders, have been particularly articulate in their social teaching. They have made daring proposals for social change, and they have offered a detailed cultural critique of Canadian society. They have been bold.

When John Paul II visited Canada in 1984 many people wondered whether the Pope would endorse the radical social teaching of the Canadian bishops. He did. He repeated verbatim, and then expanded a famous sentence of the bishops, expressing the preferential option for the poor: "The needs of the poor have priority over the wants of the rich; the rights of workers are more important than the maximization of profits; the participation of marginalized groups has precedence over the system that excludes them."

The cultural critique offered by John Paul II on his

visit to Canada concentrated on what the dominance of the market has done to people's values. Capitalism has made us into a consumer society. We dream of buying and selling, we evaluate other people in terms of what they own and consume, and we judge our own life in accordance with an economic scale of success. Science and technology are made to serve the same end, to increase economic profit, and to multiply commodities.

Modern capitalist society has transformed us into a society of individualists, utilitarians, and relativists. We are *individualists* because we have come to believe that each person must look after himself or herself. We have become self-promoters. We do not experience society as a joint project, in which we are responsible for one another. The dominance of the market has taught us that we are competitors, each responsible for his or her personal advancement.

Related to this individualism is the trend that has made us into *utilitarians*. Market relations have begun to penetrate all spheres of social life. We increasingly measure our human relations and the orientation of our life in terms of their usefulness. Do they bring us advantages? If everything must be useful, then everything has its price. Our culture is tolerant of people who espouse nonutilitarian values, such as religious devotion or love of neighbour, but dominant wisdom regards such values as private choices aimed at purely subjective satisfaction; in other words, as commodities. Human beings are by nature utility-maximizers. Dedication to the community becomes here a personal hobby taken up by those who enjoy it.

Finally, there is *relativism*. Simply put, since all values have a price, they are all relative. There is no absolute. Implied in the rejection of the absolute is a purely secular world view, without reference to transcendence. Morality is simply the adjustment to the mores of society. And since the mores of society vary, so will personal morality. Ethics is no longer a commitment to a value, a vision, and a lifestyle that stands over against society and judges it.

Because we have become individualists, utilitarians, and relativists, we have lost the sense of social solidarity, no longer believing that we belong to one another and are jointly responsible for our world. We are therefore unable to muster the political will to overcome unemployment and transform society in accordance with economic justice. As a community we have become powerless. We are unable to transform the economic system to make it serve all sectors of society .

In his speeches in Canada Pope John Paul II suggested a daring comparative analysis. In Third World countries people are economically oppressed. The great majority is excluded from the wealth of society. In the communist world of Eastern Europe, people are politically oppressed. They are deprived of their civil liberties. And in the capitalist world of the West, people are culturally oppressed. The consumerist orientation of the economy makes them powerless and thus unable to overcome unemployment and create an economy that serves the whole of society.

Yet this mainstream consumer culture, created by the dominance of the market, is not the only cultural current in modern society. We still enjoy traditions and institutions that generate a counterlanguage of solidarity and community. In his 1981 encyclical on labour, the Pope argued that the labour movement, struggling for more responsible participation in the process of production, generates a sense of social solidarity and a concern for society as a whole.

On his visit to Canada John Paul II pointed to the various religious traditions, especially Christian and Jewish, as resources for the overcoming of individualism and utilitarianism. He expressed words of admiration for the spiritual tradition of the Native Peoples, with its strong emphasis on community. He praised the French Canadian collective experience, and honoured the various ethnic communities for providing and promoting communitarian values. In his many speeches the Pope presented the movement for the defense of human rights or democracy as an important cultural force that creates a sense of community and worldwide solidarity. These, then, are cultural countercurrents: the labour movement, the religious traditions, national identity, ethnic heritage, and the quest for democracy.

Clearly, things have changed. It is well known that in the nineteenth century the Roman Catholic Church in Europe was so identified with the old regime that it repudiated the emergence of modern, liberal society. The papacy and the Church rejected the idea of democracy and civil liberties, fearing that democratic freedoms would foster relativism in regard to truth and indifference in regard to justice. By contrast, Catholics at large in the English-speaking world, mostly a minority of the population, welcomed the democratic institutions and democratic values of their societies. As for the Catholic Church, it changed its official teaching on human rights at the Second Vatican Council.

The ethical argument that proved to be of greatest importance in this change of heart was the fuller recognition of human dignity. The dignity of human persons, created in God's image, demands that they become the responsible agents of the societies and organizations to which they belong. In the language used by John Paul II, people are meant to be the "subjects" of their social world. Industrial production is alienating when the workers are prohibited from being coresponsible agents or "subjects" of production. And political society is unjust when citizens are not allowed to be "subjects," that is, to participate in the decision-making process.

But can it be said that the Catholic Church has accepted democractic values? This is a question asked by many contemporary observers with long memories. It is also asked by ecumenically minded Protestants who follow with sympathy the current renewal in the Catholic Church.

To answer this question I wish to make an important distinction. Democracy can be understood in two quite different ways, even if in our own societies they overlap. Sometimes democracy is understood as a political system that seeks to maximize personal freedom. Here it is accompanied by the ideal of minimal government intervention -- basically the freedom of people to do what they like. From this point of view, democracy encourages individualism and is in perfect harmony with a capitalist system. Yet democracy can also be understood as a political system that seeks to maximize not personal freedom but personal participation. Here it is seen as an institutional development enhancing people's ability to share in the decisions that affect their lives and the life of the whole community. Democracy interpreted in this manner engenders a strong sense of solidarity. If democracy is seen as maximizing participation, it is at odds with a capitalist system that allows only the owners or directors, but never the workers, to share in the decision-making process.

As for whether Catholic social teaching has endorsed the democratic tradition, I can now deal with the question. If democracy is understood as maximizing personal freedom, then the answer is No. But if democracy is understood as maximizing the participation of the many in the decisions made by the few, then the answer is Yes. This is the concept of democracy John Paul II has in mind when he praises the institutional defense of human rights. And the human rights, as defined by him, include the right to allow humans to be free and responsible agents in their society. The quest for greater democracy in this sense is a counter-trend to individualism, generating social solidarity.

However trenchant his analysis of society has been, it has not escaped notice that John Paul II has until now been unwilling to apply his teaching to the Catholic Church itself. For in the Catholic Church the members are also destined to be "subjects" or responsible participants. The inherited papal-episcopal structure of the Catholic Church in no way impedes the creation of institutions that allow participation and coresponsibility. As a matter of fact, the Second Vatican Council in the sixties was just such an important institutional event that allowed many-levelled participation in the Catholic Church.

Allow me to add that this is a point that not only concerns Catholics but touches the wider community. Why? Because the self-organizing of a church has cultural power. The form church government takes teaches church members how to interact, how important decisions are to be made, how to assume collective responsibility -- and in doing so, it promotes an ethical ideal for the whole of society. The Protestant churches have been powerful cultural forces promoting democracy by the way in which they have engaged their own members and called for their responsible participation on every level. By contrast, in the past, the authoritarian self-organization of the Catholic Church has created cultural sympathy for authoritarian, nondemocratic forms of secular rule.

Today, the official teaching of the Catholic Church fosters human rights and responsible participation in society. But can it communicate these new values to society if the ecclesiastical organization itself fails to integrate responsible participation in decision-making? The Catholic bishops of the United States wrestled with this question in their 1986 pastoral on economic justice. They recognized the Church as "a significant cultural actor." And they put it this way: "As we have proposed a new experiment in collaboration and participation in decision-making by all those affected on all levels of U.S. society, so we the bishops also commit the Church to become a model of collaboration and participation."

In the last analysis, the struggle over justice has to do (a) with material things, with bread, jobs, and the distribution of wealth and power, and (b) with spiritual things, with the cultural symbols that express the ethos of society. The struggle for justice therefore has a political and a cultural dimension. In the last analysis it is a conflict over values. The churches lament the individualism and utilitarianism produced by the dominance of the market because these values promote a culture that undermines social solidarity and makes people politically powerless. Of course, the churches also recognize counter-trends in society that generate communitarian values and a sense of collective responsibility. These counter-trends are fostered by the religious and ethnic traditions, the labour movement and political action to promote democratic participation. The bold social transformation that is required will not come about unless these various groups, as bearers of community values, succeed in organizing themselves as a movement of solidarity.

There is something special about the present historical moment. John Paul II and the Canadian Catholic bishops have argued that the world economic system has come to a crisis point. They claim that we may have reached the end point of the more benign phase of capitalism, created after the Great Depression by Keynesian economics and New Deal legislation, or its equivalent in the nations of the West. What we are witnessing today is a hardening of the capitalist system.

The World Council of Churches and many Protestant

church leaders have arrived at the same conclusion. But the Canadian bishops have taken the analysis one step further. They argue that what is being dissolved at this time is the unwritten contract between the power elite and society in general, a contract forged after World War Two, in favour of full employment, welfare legislation, and respect for labour organizations.

In fact, it is precisely the growth of unemployment and poverty, the decline of public support for those in need, and the concerted effort to weaken or even destroy organized labour that have provoked the Canadian Catholic bishops and the leaders of the other Christian churches to become more outspoken in their social teaching. They have opted for solidarity with the people at the bottom and in the margin. A similar response to present economic conditions has taken place in the American churches.

What deserves to be mentioned in this context is that the present shift in economic orientation is accompanied by a neo-conservative set of values, a trend that tries to legitimate the present reorientation and give the power elite a good conscience despite the widening gap between rich and poor. Quebeckers refer to this trend more correctly as *"neo-libéral."* Since every economic system, or every modification of an economic system, is in need of a culture that blesses it, it is not surprising that the present tightening up of capitalism is endorsed by an appropriate set of hardhearted values.

After World War Two the labour movement and progressive governments were able to control the capitalist economy to a certain extent. The wealth produced began to reach people even at the lowest level. And this was accompanied by a cultural consensus recognizing certain collective values, such as the overcoming of social inequality and economic security for all. Even the economic elite accepted the utility of these values. Reactionary groups that opposed them had to defend their own plans for society in words that appeared to respect them. Over several decades, all political parties advertised their programs in terms of the beneficial impact these would have on the great majority of the people.

But there are many signs, the Canadian bishops argue, that this discourse has come to an end.

Today we are told that we have lived beyond our means, that society has been overly generous, that we have given away money, and that, accordingly, the government deficit is the central problem of the economy. We must recognize, we are told, that we live in the tough world of competition. We must advance our economy by letting private enterprise be the locomotive that pulls us out of the present slump.

We hear that the successful entrepreneurs are the creators of wealth. That is why they deserve the assistance of government, tax breaks, and subsidies, along with the riches they make for themselves. The reason that our industries are not competitive on the world market is that labourers ask for excessive wages. The unions have become too powerful. There are too many strikes. It is their fault that we suffer economic decline. We all will have to tighten our belts -- all, one assumes, except the creators of wealth. An increase of unemployment has become inevitable. Computer technology is beginning to replace many jobs. At fault also are the women and the immigrants who have recently joined the labour force. As long as the unemployment rate is "normal" -- which is a term that contemporary economists use for something that has the rest of us puzzled -- we will have to get used to it. This is not the time for free lunches. Government should no longer assume responsibility for people who cannnot make it in a society that gives them every opportunity. What we need are volunteer organizations, such as churches and missions, to offer a helping hand to the poor in our society. A certain toughness has become necessary to make labour work harder, to encourage business confidence and to attract foreign investment.

The neo-conservative cultural trend that I have been describing makes selfishness respectable. Am I my brother's keeper? According to the prevailing mood, the answer is No. It is all right to let the social gap become wider. There is no need anymore even to pretend that social solidarity counts.

In the United States and Great Britain these neo-conservative values are allied to other cultural currents, a new kind of nationalism, nostalgic of past glories, a heightening of the Cold War rhetoric, what I would consider an ideological attachment to capitalism as a system beyond criticism, and a tough philosophy of national security that blesses state violence, nuclear weapons, arms production, and increased policing of society.

What is puzzling in these circumstances is the new stress on purely personal ethical standards. Ethics, according to this view, is a guide for individuals, not for the social order. Ethics, from this point of view, has nothing to do with the manner in which people organize their economic life. Political leaders are thus judged in terms of their private morality -- how many shoes a politician has in the closet -- not in terms of the morality of their public policies.

There are Christian preachers, especially on television, who back up this ethical individualism by offering a purely personal understanding of the biblical message. In other words, the Bible does nothing more than save individuals, one by one, from the common destruction. According to them, the Gospel generates private virtue, not social justice. The government deserves support when it promotes private virtue, but should be opposed when it tries to establish ethical norms for public affairs, such as limitation of arms production, the reduction of nuclear weapons, assistance to Third World countries, the protection of the environment, and the containment of the free market.

Admittedly, Canada has a different political history. We have never been an empire. We have never made free enterprise an ideology. For this reason the kind of neo-conservatism I have been analyzing is much weaker in Canadian society. Many Canadians, including many church groups, have argued against free trade with the United States because they fear that economic integration will bring with it cultural assimilation and undermine the communitarian and social values Canadians have inherited. They fear that we will we lose the identity that sustains our social programs and our social democratic tradition.

Well, we live in an age of fear. As the circle of prosperity and security is shrinking, people on all social levels become more afraid. Scarcity creates fear and anger. These feelings affect people who are unemployed, and they also affect people who hold insecure jobs, or who suffer a decline of income, or who have to work much harder to make a living. Almost all of us are worried about the future, struggling for our own survival, and often, possibly without noticing it, we begin to shrug our shoulders about the rest of society. Unless it is resisted by an involving political movement, scarcity inevitably produces more selfishness. We want to protect our own advantage.

In spite of our different political history, we need not flatter ourselves that Canada will remain more generous than other nations. Just take the irrational reaction of Canadian society, encouraged by the government, to the recent arrival of refugee groups. As a result, the government has tightened our borders with new legislation.

However, what impresses me is that the reactionary trend encounters substantial resistance in Canadian society. The neo-conservative values are opposed by many circles, groups, and organizations in this country. A countermovement is in the making that defines itself in terms of social solidarity, with the Canadian churches making their own contribution to it. It is in fact quite remarkable that in Canada and even in the United States, all the mainline Christian churches have, in their public statements, opposed the neo-conservative values. This does not mean, of course, that the people in the pews have followed them. Nevertheless the leadership is there. And the primary argument of the churches against the growing hardness of contemporary society has been staunchly ethical. For example, with regard to the refugee problem in particular, all the Canadian churches and synagogues got together and prepared a counter-proposal for an alternative legislation and submitted it to the government. Ethics, biblical ethics, recognizes the dignity of human beings and demands that economic and political institutions be of service to them. Morality, the churches argue, calls for social solidarity. Ethics demands that a society organize itself in such a way that all its members participate in production and that all have their basic needs supplied.

It is obvious that the churches don't just moralize. They are not naïve, claiming that if we all become more generous or more loving then our economic problems will disappear. What they say instead is that we need structural change in the economic order and that this can be brought about only as we as a society opt for compassion and solidarity.

This is an important point. We are so used to hearing the churches preach morality that we easily mishear their social message. Even in parishes and at other church gatherings, people often have the impression that the new teaching demands of them and of society a higher morality. But high-mindedness will not solve the unemployment problem. What the church leaders are saying is that what we need are structural changes in the economic order, that might mean, for instance, worker ownership or community ownership or other alternative forms of economic development -- and then the churchmen add that this political task can be achieved only through an ethical commitment to solidarity.

The future of Canadian society, and the future of the world, depends on the outcome of this conflict over values. That the Christian Church in this country and in many parts of the world, especially the Third World, should join this struggle in support of social compassion and solidarity is a remarkable historical development.

For centuries and centuries the major churches, Catholic and Protestant, have tended to side with the powerful, with the dominant sector of society. In the Third World the churches have supported colonialism. Some critics say this recent change of heart, this religious conversion, finds expression only on paper, in ecclesiastical documents, and represents only an insignificant minority of Christians. The churches that make these bold declarations, the critics say, do not follow them up with actions.

There is some truth in these critical remarks. It is easier to write a daring position paper than to carry it out. At the same time, the explosion of solidarity in the churches represents a profound spiritual transformation, a new experience of God, a renewal of fidelity to the Gospel, and hence a development that has great spiritual authority in the churches. The new movement linking faith and justice will not dwindle away: it will become stronger. And as society becomes harsher, it will thrive on the challenge.

Bibliographical Note

John William's *Canadian Churches and Social Justice* (Toronto: Lorimer, 1984) is a useful collection of recent church documents dealing with social justice issues. For the evolution of Roman Catholic social teaching, see Donal Dorr, *Option for the Poor: A Hundred Years of Vatican Social Teaching* (Maryknoll, N.Y.: Orbis Books, 1983). The social messages of the Canadian Catholic bishops can be found in E.F. Sheridan, *Do Justice!* (Toronto: Jesuit Centre for Social Faith and Justice, 1987). For an analysis of these texts see G. Baum, D. Cameron, *Ethics and Economics* (Toronto: Lorimer, 1984) and G. Baum's *Theology and Society* (New York: Paulist Press, 1987). The most celebrated expression of Latin American liberation theology is Gustavo Gutierrez, *A Theology of Liberation* (Maryknoll, N.Y.: Orbis Books, 1973).

The CBC Massey Lectures Series

The Politics of the Family
R. D. Laing
0-88784-546-0 (p)

The Educated Imagination
Northrop Frye
0-88784-598-3 (p)

The Real World of Democracy
C. B. Macpherson
0-88784-530-4 (p)

Available in fine bookstores and at www.anansi.ca